Franco's death in November 1975 ended one of the most famous single-handed "reigns" in history. For a third of a century Franco was Spain and Spain was Franco. Some regarded him as a cruel dictator who enforced a harsh repressive regime; to others he was the saviour of Spain.

Franco was a professional soldier. What he lacked in education and political experience he made up for with determination and ambition. After the famous meeting between Franco and Adolf Hitler in October 1940 Hitler is reported to have said that he would rather have two teeth out than go through it again. So what was this shrewd, calculating, reserved man really like?

The story of Franco's rise and final emergence as *el Caudillo,* or leader, of Spain is both exciting and horrific. Richard Kisch tells how Franco re-united his country after it had been torn apart by the bitter and bloody struggle of civil war. He describes how, despite economic hardships and quarrels with his own party, Franco firmly established and maintained his iron grip on Spanish fortunes until his death. As this book reveals, his was a quite remarkable career. This book has more than forty illustrations, a glossary, a list of principal characters, a reading list, a table of dates and an index.

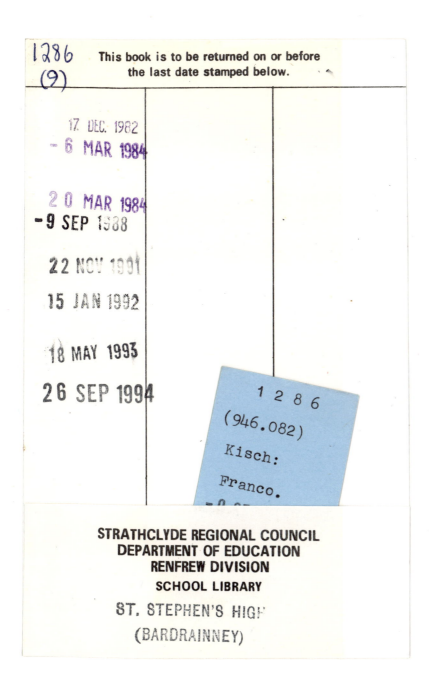

WAYLAND HISTORY MAKERS

Franco

Richard Kisch

WAYLAND PUBLISHERS LIMITED

More Wayland History Makers

The Last Czar W. H. C. Smith
Picasso David Sweetman
Goering F. H. Gregory
Adolf Hitler Matthew Holden
Al Capone Mary Letts
The Wright Brothers Russell Ash
Karl Marx Caroline Seaward
Lenin Lionel Kochan
Rommel F. H. Gregory
Jomo Kenyatta Julia Friedmann
Martin Luther King Patricia Baker
Captain Scott David Sweetman
Bismarck Richard Kisch
Joseph Stalin David Hayes and F. H. Gregory
Cecil Rhodes Neil Bates
Cromwell Amanda Purves
The Borgias David Sweetman
Mao Tse-Tung Hugh Purcell

Frontispiece General Franco
(1892-1975).

SBN 85340 302 3
Copyright © 1976 by Wayland (Publishers) Ltd
49 Lansdowne Place, Hove, East Sussex BN3 1HS
First published in 1977 by
Wayland Publishers Ltd

Printed in Great Britain by Biddles Ltd, Guildford, Surrey

Contents

1. The General Gets His Feet Wet

In July 1936 a British de Havilland *Dragon Rapide* aircraft flew into the sun over the Canary Islands, circled and asked permission to land at the Las Palmas airstrip. The plane had been chartered in London. Señor Luis Bolin, an influential Spanish journalist of *ABC,* a right-wing Spanish newspaper, had organized the flight. He was helped by Douglas Jerrold, a British journalist and well-known Catholic publicist. Bolin moved in High Society and had a reputation as a bit of a playboy, so there was nothing strange about his departure for a quiet weekend in Morocco. An old friend, a former British army major, went with him. So did a couple of girls. The pilot, Captain Cecil Bebb, MC, was a former British Airforce officer from the First World War.

As soon as the plane had touched down at Casablanca there was an apparent change of plan. Captain Bebb was asked whether he would take the plane on to the Canary Islands. He agreed. But Señor Bolin stayed behind. Once the aircraft landed at Las Palmas, the other passengers disembarked. They had served their purpose as a screen for Señor Bolin, and disappeared from the story. After they left the plane was immediately boarded by an armed guard of Spanish soldiers. The officer in command saluted the pilot and invited him, firmly but politely, to follow.

Captain Bebb was escorted under guard to a villa on the hillside above Las Palmas, where he was told that he would be required to fly a Very Important Person to

Opposite page General Franco pictured at about the time he led the rebel forces in the revolt that eventually resulted in his becoming Dictator of Spain.

an un-named destination. Until then he was invited to enjoy the comfort and quiet hospitality of the villa. Some hours later, in the early morning, Captain Bebb was woken up and escorted back to his aircraft. He found it had been serviced, refuelled and wheeled out to the blind side of the airport. Still under guard, he was ordered to be ready to leave at a moment's notice. But on no account was the starter to be used until he was instructed. Bebb made himself comfortable, and waited. Not far away, the waiting VIP was putting up a display of cool self-control. He was a tubby, short-legged military man of some forty-three years. He had a scrubby toothbrush-moustache under a firm but not over-prominent hook nose. He was spending his time drafting and correcting documents from his briefcase.

Right Franco was at first extremely cautious about joining the rebellion. Once he had decided in favour of the conspiracy, however, he did not hesitate — his motto was "Blind faith in Victory".

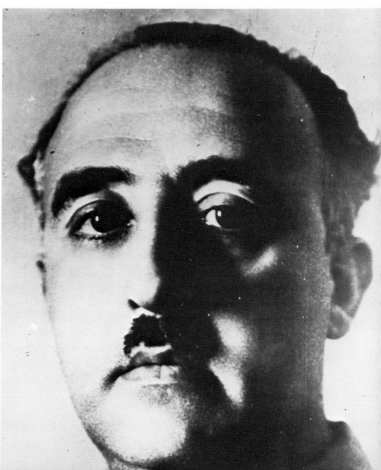

His name was Francisco Paulino Hermanguildo Teoduldo Franco y Bahamonde. More simply, he was General Franco, Captain-General of the Spanish Forces in the Canary Islands.

General Franco had already made decisive moves for the future. He had packed off his wife and daughter on a German liner. They were to stay with friends in Hamburg. Taking advantage of the sudden death of his old friend, General Balmes, the military governor of the Grand Canaries, Franco had slipped away from his own headquarters on the islands, at Teneriffe. He had come to Las Palmas for the funeral.

General Balmes, it seemed, had shot himself the day before. Was it meant as a warning? Or had it been a patriot's desperate last act when faced with the impossible choice between his political preferences and his national obligations?

General Franco had not hesitated. As soon as the funeral was over he had returned to a suite on the first floor of the Hotel Madrid to await the next move. It came—at three o'clock in the morning on 18th July, 1936. Franco's cousin, Salgado, came into the General's room with a message. It was a telegram from Melilla, Command Headquarters of the Spanish Army of Africa. It was addressed to General Franco. The message read:

GENERAL SOLANS TO GENERAL FRANCO: ARMY RISEN IN ARMS AGAINST GOVERNMENT. ALL INSTRUMENTS OF COMMAND SEIZED. VIVA ESPANA!

The next two hours were hectic. General Franco had become the central figure of a conspiracy against the Republican Government in Spain. Orders and messages flashed in from all over the Spanish North African colonies and the mainland. They arrived one after the other at the hotel room in Las Palmas. Each message was signed with the code sequence *"Fe ciego en el triumfo!"*—"Blind faith in victory!"

9

At Franco's demand, the conspirators acknowledged him as the supreme military commander of the army of Africa in revolt. He then had an order telegraphed to all Spanish garrison commanders in North Africa:

"All Glory to the heroic African Army! Spain above all! Receive our enthusiastic salutation all those garrisons who unite themselves to you and other companions in the peninsula in these heroic moments. Blind Faith in Victory! Long Live Spain with Honour!"

General Franco was then escorted to a small motor fishing boat that was moored out of sight of the harbour. Making a large sweep out to sea, it approached the airstrip from the seaward side to avoid observation. In the aircraft, Captain Bebb received instructions to prepare for take-off as soon as the sound of the approaching motor vessel had been identified. He was also told to head for Tetuan in Morocco. Busy revving up the engine, he did little more than glance at the small podgy man in uniform clambering aboard the aircraft. The newcomer's trousers were wringing wet. Apparently the approach on the seaboard side of the airstrip was too shallow. The motor vessel had gone aground. The Very Important Person had had to jump for it and had landed short and got his feet wet in the process.

When Bebb next looked up, the VIP was in his underpants. He had quietly stripped off his uniform and folded it neatly. Later it was jettisoned from the plane with other material. The influential passenger was leaving nothing to chance. He took a conventional civilian suit from the leather bag he had brought on board and dressed quickly. Later he was reported to have used Arab dress to disguise himself more thoroughly.

As soon as he was satisfied with his appearance, Bebb's passenger came forward to the pilot's seat. He held out his hand as he introduced himself: "I am General Franco," he said with a marked Spanish accent. He smiled and then returned to his seat. He took a document from his briefcase and began reading it carefully. It was the original of the proclamation at that moment being relayed over the air from the rebel broadcasting station at Melilla. It was the first manifesto to be issued by the miscellaneous group of rebel generals. It called on the army to rise in arms against the lawfully appointed government of the Republic, elected the previous February. The opening phrases echoed General Franco's sincere, personal dedication and sense of purpose:

"Spaniards! All those of you who feel a holy love of Spain; all those in the ranks of the Army and Navy, who have made an act of profession in the service of the Motherland; those who have sworn to defend her against her enemies, until Death, the Nation calls you in her defence. . . ."

Left Franco in military uniform, his usual dress. During the early days of the rebellion he is reported to have disguised himself in Arab dress in order to keep his movements completely secret.

2. The Quiet Professional

In July 1936, General Francisco Franco was one of Spain's top soldiers. But it was far from certain then, that within three months he would emerge as the acknowledged leader of the group of anti-republican generals responsible for a war which drenched Spain in blood for nearly three years from 1936-1939. The conflict began as a civil war with Spaniard fighting Spaniard but it also had far-reaching international consequences.

In these early years General Franco was not widely known outside his own country. Instead the man who had been tipped as the likely leader of army resistance to the Republic was General José Sanjurjo, a rough tough ex-colonial warrior known as the "Lion of the Riffs". Sanjurjo was the former commander of the Spanish forces in Morocco who, in the early 1920s, were still engaged in the long drawn-out war against nationalists holding out in the Riff mountains. He was waiting in exile in Portugal, hoping to take over the leadership of the 1936 revolt. His bags were packed. He was expecting to fly back on the wings of the rebellion to be installed in Madrid as the leader of a new fascist state with which the generals intended to replace the Spanish Republic.

Franco had taken his time before deciding to join the conspiracy against the Republic. He was a cool, cautious and careful man. He was also intensely ambitious, a fact that his critics among Republican leaders had already made much of. But he lacked glamour and physical presence. Among his fellow

> "To know my flag is waving over Spain while I am listening to the music of the Royal March, makes me want to die." *General José Sanjurjo, July 1936, on the eve of his ill-fated flight.*

12

conspirators Franco was not as clever as Emilio Mola, known as *The Fox,* the organizing brain behind the plot; nor did he have the bluster and vulgarity of Queipo de Llano, the barnstorming Inspector-General of Customs who virtually seized Seville for the rebels single-handed. He had little of the fanaticism of the sinister Millan Astray, the one-eyed, one-armed commander of the notorious Tercio Corps, the storm troopers of the Spanish Foreign Legion. And unlike his old comrade-in-arms, General Manuel Goded, then Captain-General of the Balearic Islands, he was not an aristocrat.

Francisco Franco was a quiet man. He was content to be regarded as a professional soldier and a good officer. But he shrewdly made the most of the implied distinction that he was a *professional* rather than a politician and this fact masked his unshakeable determination to get to the top. It took him from Lieutenant to General before he was thirty. Physically he was a broad-shouldered, stocky figure, only just over five feet tall. He was also going thin on top.

General Franco was born on 4th December, 1882. His family lived at El Ferrol, near Corunna, on the Atlantic coast. It was Spain's most important naval base and arsenal at the northwest tip of the Iberian Peninsula. It was a typical service town with rigid social attitudes and sharply drawn class divisions. The staff and administrative sections of the arsenal came lower in the social scale than members of the active naval establishment. Franco's father, Nicolas, like his father before him, was on the administrative staff of the arsenal in the pay corps. He was an assistant paymaster.

Nicolas was also a gambler and a drinker whose love affairs had become a family scandal. As a result Señora Franco, his estranged wife, had taken complete charge of the up-bringing of their five children. She

> "Ignacio had always said that Franco was a very ambitious man—General Goded was more intelligent; General Mola a better soldier; but Franco was the most ambitious." *Constancia de la Mora,* In Place of Splendour.

13

dominated their education and tried to instill in them her devout religious beliefs.

Francisco was clearly much influenced by his mother although he did not share her views on religion. His younger brother Ramon, however, was quite different. He broke away from his mother's apron strings as soon as he could and joined the airforce. He became a hero in the early 1920s as the first Spanish pilot to make a single-handed transatlantic flight to Argentina. He also dabbled in politics and was implicated in the military intrigues which contributed to the fall of the Spanish monarchy and the abdication of King Alfonso XIII in 1931.

Francisco took a different attitude. He had been very embarrassed by Ramon's political adventuring. His

Below Franco's younger brother Ramon was involved in many of the plots that contributed to the fall of the Spanish monarchy and the abdication of King Alfonso XIII in 1931. This picture shows the scene after a bomb had been thrown at Alfonso on his wedding day — 31st May, 1906.

temperament was subdued and sullen and he showed no inclination to copy his father's love for high living. His chief concern was to get out of the restricting family connection with the pay corps. Above all he wanted to strike a patriotic blow to restore the prestige of his country.

Throughout Franco's childhood Spain was nursing her bruises after the disasters she had experienced at the turn of the century. Spain had lost the few remaining traces of her former imperial glory in Latin America. She had been thrown out of Cuba, as well as the Philippines during the Spanish-American war in 1898. Also the Spanish fleet, with its timber ships and muzzle-loading guns had been swept off the high seas by the United States navy.

Below Throughout Franco's childhood Spain had experienced many disasters. In 1898 she lost the Philippines during the Spanish-American war. This picture shows the US *City of Peking* leaving San Francisco with reinforcements, bound for the Philippines.

Franco was only six at the time of these defeats but he was determined to avenge them by joining the navy. But when the time came, as a result of cuts and re-organization, the intake to the Naval Academy was reduced and Franco's application rejected. Instead he had to content himself with the Infantry Training College at Toledo.

In 1910, Franco graduated. He was under eighteen and the youngest in his class. He was commissioned as a Lieutenant and posted to garrison duty but found it very routine and dull. Franco began looking for action. He found it in North Africa where Spain was attempting to grab some colonial territory. During the First World War Spain's new colonialists sought to strengthen their position in Morocco's Riff mountains. This was the stronghold of the nationalist leader, Abd-el-Krim.

Franco was posted to Africa in 1912. He applied to join the élite *Regulares,* a special colonial general service unit of police and regular soldiers. It was the forerunner of the Spanish Foreign Legion which was founded in 1923 on the French model. He was quickly promoted and became a Captain before he was twenty-two. Franco was not notably popular amongst his fellow officers and had few intimate friends. But he was popular with his troops and looked after their welfare. He did not try to avoid any fighting and was frequently in the front line. On one occasion a thermos flask was shot out of his hand as he raised the cup to drink. His reaction was rather pompous: "God has given us life and only God can take it". In 1916 he was wounded in the stomach but returned to the front line as soon as he was fit. He was promoted to Major and nicknamed "The Little Major" by his men. He was then only twenty-three years old.

Franco was beginning to get a clearer idea of his mission. Years later he told an interviewer: *"La guera*

Below Abd-el-Krim, leader of the Riffs.

era lo mio!", which means "War is my destiny. I was sure of that!" He had another four years campaigning in the field before being transferred to home duty. He was appointed commander of the Oviedo garrison in the Asturias not far from his home town. But he was still uncomfortable. He did not fit into the conventional social pattern of local provincial life. But at this time he met his future wife, Carmen Polo, the daughter of a wealthy industrialist. She helped steady him socially and smoothed out some of his rougher edges. But he had a disappointment when he applied to take a course at the army staff college. He was told that he was "too senior," although he was still only twenty-three.

Franco's big chance came in 1921. He returned to Morocco for what was intended to be the last round-up of the rebels under Abd-el-Krim. Instead it almost turned into the final stand of the Foreign Legion. The Spanish forces were thrashed and forced back around Melilla. When the commander of the Legion was killed, Franco took over. He was promoted on the spot to Lieutenant-Colonel and not long afterwards he was made a full Colonel. His commanding officer, a General Sartos, referred to him in despatches as "brilliant". He was praised for his combat successes, courage, competence, skill and serenity. "His brilliant actions in combat," wrote the General, "were a summary of his exceptional qualities."

This was the period when Franco established and consolidated his friendship with the army colleagues who were later to play crucial roles in supporting him on his way to the supreme leadership of Spain. They included virtually every leading general in the future fascist state.

3. The King's Favourite

Spain in 1936 was still one of the most backward, least developed countries in Europe. It was fenced off from the rest of Europe by the Pyrenees mountains and had escaped the challenges of commercial expansion and industrialization. Throughout the nineteenth century Spain had been subject to a continuous series of wars, internal upheavals and conflicts. It had been devastated during the French revolutionary wars when Napoleon Bonaparte tried to put his brother, Joseph, on the throne. The Spanish monarchy had finally been restored in 1814 as a constitutional regime but came under the rule of the reactionary Ferdinand VII. There was an unsuccessful revolution in 1820. Ferdinand's daughter Isabella succeeded him at his death in 1833, but she was deposed in 1868. Fighting between the Carlists, royalist supporters of the pretender, Don Carlos, and republicans followed. However, in 1874 Isabella's son was proclaimed King as Alfonso XII and mainly through the skills of his ministers his reign of eleven years was a time of relative prosperity for Spain.

Under Alfonso XIII (1886-1941) however, there were further constitutional crises with the powers of the Cortes (the Spanish parliament) restricted by a limited, highly qualified franchise, and powerful opposition from the church. There was constant growing pressure from Republican elements as well as developing influence from socialist and anarchist movements. The unity of the Kingdom was also continually at risk from the strong regional movements particularly among the Catalans, the Basques, the Galicians and Andalusians.

Opposite page, top King Ferdinand VII of Spain (1784-1833). He became King in 1814, when the Spanish monarchy was restored as a constitutional regime.

Opposite page, below left Queen Isabella II of Spain (1830-1904). The daughter of Ferdinand VII, she was deposed in 1868.

Opposite page, below right King Alfonso XII of Spain (1857-1885). The son of Isabella II, he was proclaimed King in 1874. His reign of eleven years was a time of relative prosperity for Spain.

In terms of twentieth-century development Spain was still semi-feudal. Some 50,000 landowners held enormous power in the countryside, while thousands of aristocrats and absentee landlords never went near their property. Over 67 per cent of all the land was in the hands of 2 per cent of the population. Nearly 70 per cent of the population lived in conditions of absolute misery and poverty. They knew few luxuries. The peasants lived on cabbage soup and beans and very rarely ate meat. Their poultry and eggs were strictly for selling in the market but only brought them a few pesetas.

The conditions of the vast majority of peasants (*braceros*) were notorious. They were treated like serfs by the landlords and their *caiques,* the foremen and bailiffs. They were pushed around by the *Guardia civilia,* the police, and dominated and directed by the Church. Death had become a Spanish preoccupation. It was glorified by the Church, and glamorized by the excitement and rituals of the bullring.

Industry was limited and widely scattered in Catalonia, in the east, or the Basque provinces of the west. The biggest coal, iron and mineral deposits were in the Asturias mountains. There was copper at Rio Tinto. Many of Spain's natural resources and mineral wealth were controlled by foreign investors, particularly in Britain and western Europe. There were huge deposits of cobalt, nickel, titanium and wolfram which had barely been touched. But Spain was subject to the same economic pressures, industrial strife and social conflict as the rest of Europe in the years of tension which followed the First World War. Spain's industrial workers were as aware as workers elsewhere in Europe of the rise of revolutionary forces, not to mention the challenge of a new social order in Soviet Russia. Their conditions of work, low wages, long hours, and the determined opposition of employers to all forms of trade union organization, were even worse than those in most other European countries.

An army general, Don Miguel Primo de Rivera, the Marqués de Estella, moved to establish himself as the Spanish strong-man behind the monarchy. He pushed the King, Alfonso XIII, into the background and imposed a dictatorship under the monarchy.

General Primo de Rivera became dictator of Spain in 1923. This was also the year that Francisco Franco married Carmen Polo.

Below King Alfonso XIII (front right) (1886-1941). On his right is General Primo de Rivera, who became Dictator of Spain in 1923.

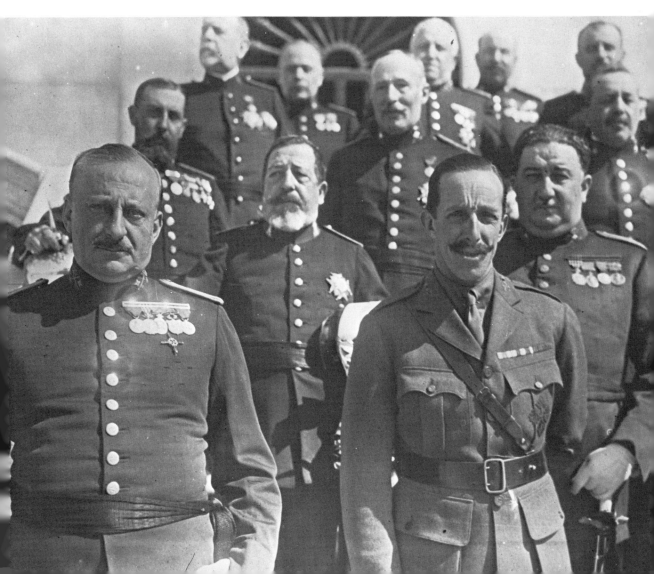

Below King Alfonso XIII was the "puppet" of the Dictator Primo de Rivera. He attempted to win over Franco as a possible ally, but in the crisis of 1931 Franco did nothing to prevent the forced abdication of the King.

In contrast to what was happening to the regime, marriage was good for the young colonel. He became noticeably more relaxed and socially self-confident. He even began to show a small talent for literature. Later, after producing a couple of novelettes and a film script using a family name, da Costa, as a *nom-de-plume,* he was able to ensure his rise to the Spanish Academy of Letters. At the same time he also made the occasional speech, though he showed little real talent as a public speaker. It was obvious that Dona Carmen had taken firm charge of the family set-up. She smartened up her husband's social image and placed the family firmly in respectable social upper-class circles.

At the same time, Franco himself was becoming increasingly noticed as one of the rising stars of the army. He commanded the army's élite force in the field during the final stages of the Moroccan campaign. He was also being significantly singled out for special marks of favour by King Alfonso. It had not escaped notice that when the King and Queen Ena paid a visit to Morocco in October 1923, the King had especially asked that Franco be invited to escort them.

King Alfonso was in a difficult position. He was increasingly isolated from the mass of the people and was encircled by the rigid court traditions of the Escorial Palace in Madrid. As an individual he was a rather weak, ineffectual person. He was virtually the last survivor of the doomed Habsburg dynasty which had once controlled the whole of Europe from the Netherlands to Austria, Hungary and Italy. He had the characteristic Habsburg lower lip—almost his only legacy from the family's great imperial past. He had married Queen Victoria's grand-daughter, Ena, but that alliance carried little weight in the Europe that emerged after the First World War. Belatedly he was beginning to show some awareness of the difficulty of his position as the *puppet* of the dictator. He started to look for possible allies in the army to provide a counterbalance to the pressures being exerted by the new master of the country.

In March 1925, the King again singled out Franco, by sending him a religious medal blessed by a celebrated Spanish saint. It was accompanied by a personal letter, using the informal pronoun "tu", a word rarely used by royalty. The King wrote: "Please wear this medal—so military and Spanish—which will surely protect you. Know how much your very affectionate friend loves and appreciates you". It was signed simply, "Alfonso XIII".

Franco had particularly distinguished himself that year during the joint French-Spanish operation, when he was co-operating with Marshal Pétain. His friend, Manuel Goded, who was also with him, reported on Franco's "modesty and dash". But there was one awkward moment of some significance in view of later developments. It involved the Colonel in a personal clash of wills with the dictator over the final assault on the Riffs. Primo de Rivera insisted it was both foolhardy and useless to attempt a final assault across the Bay at Alchuenas. But Franco insisted, and got a further proof of the King's appreciation as his reward.

In 1926, the year before General Sanjurjo was able to announce the final defeat of Abd-el-Krim, the King issued a special decree promoting Colonel Franco to the rank of Brigadier General. At thirty-three he was now not only the youngest General in Spain, but in the whole of Europe. He was also a Commander of the French Legion of Honour and had twice been awarded the Military Medal of Spain. He was also to be appointed a Lord of the King's Bedchamber.

In 1927, Franco was appointed head of the new General Military Academy that was to be opened at Saragossa. Its purpose was to transform the Spanish army and lay the foundations for an entirely new force

"Please wear this medal—so military, so Spanish—which will surely protect you. You know how much your affectionate friend loves and appreciates you." *King Alfonso XIII to Colonel Francisco Franco, March 1925.*

"1. Love your country and be loyal to the King;
2. Honour the military *esprit de corps;*
3. Be chivalrous;
4. Obey orders, faithfully;
5. Never complain;
6. Seek respect from inferiors; appreciation from superiors;
7. Accept sacrifice;
8. Comradeship above self;
9. Never shirk responsibility, make decisions;
10. Combine courage with abnegation."
Franco's Code, based on Foreign Legion Credo of General Millan Astray.

Above A parade of officers and men in training at the Military Academy in Saragossa. Franco was appointed head of the Academy in 1927.

free of the local prejudices and regional loyalties which had crippled it for many years. He was made responsible for creating a new modern army dedicated solely to the defence and protection of Spain's over-riding national interests.

The following year the young General made his first and only visit abroad. He went to Germany and inspected a training school for the future Nazi army at Leipzig. When he came back, one of his first acts was to take out a subscription to an antisocialist, anticommunist, intelligence news service. Spain's dictator was in difficulties at the time and the monarchy was obviously in decline. When Primo de Rivera tried to recruit Franco to support a coup against the King to promote his own position, Franco declined to join. Not long afterwards, Primo de Rivera himself was forced to resign. Six months later he died of a heart attack. The King publicly embraced Franco only a few weeks after the dictator's death when he was visiting the Saragossa Academy. During the visit he presented the cadets with medals bearing his effigy, and conferred on the Academy the right to fly his personal royal standard. This was one of his last official acts. A few months later, in 1931, King Alfonso and his family formally abdicated the throne. Nobody made a move to save him. Franco conspicuously stood aside and his friend left the country. Ten years later, in 1941, ex-King Alfonso XIII died in exile.

Below After King Alfonso XIII abdicated in 1931, the Royal Palaces were opened to the Spanish people and turned into museums. This photograph shows an aerial view of the Royal Palace in Madrid.

4. Enter the Republic

General Franco kept his head when a Republic came to Spain for the second time. The almost forgotten first Republic, of 1873, had only lasted twelve months. At least the second was able to survive for five years.

In 1931 there were no obvious alternative candidates to replace Primo de Rivera as the strong-man capable of supporting the monarchy or taking over himself as a one-man ruler on the lines of the Italian fascist leader, Benito Mussolini. Franco, then, was neither ready nor willing. He was a career officer with strong monarchist loyalties. His future, and his fortune, seemed to be bound up with his behaviour and relationships with his political superiors. He was also not the sort of person to risk everything on a rash gamble. The General was steering clear of backroom intrigues (*camarillas*) and conspiracies. He had also rejected an approach by the crafty Emilio Mola, then a colonel, and Director of Army Intelligence. He had taken care to divert the suspicions of Republicans, who clearly doubted his loyalty, by letting it be known that he had written a strong letter to his brother Ramon rebuking him for meddling in politics.

The Republicans then took the initiative. When the King stepped down in face of mounting economic and political pressure the constitutional vacuum was filled by an alliance of liberals. They included thinkers, writers, lawyers, university teachers, right wing socialists and miscellaneous radicals as well as the leaders of the widely-based regional movements. These had always been particularly strong among the Basque

Below Franco kept clear of all the political intrigue in Spain during the early days of the Republic. He was not prepared to risk his future until he could be sure of success.

people and the Catalans, whose sense of historic identity and dignity had been constantly repressed by the central authorities in Madrid. They were not even allowed to write or speak their own languages under the monarchy. Similar groups existed in the central and southern regions as well as in Galicia, Franco's home province. This may also have been a factor affecting Franco's behaviour though he never seems to have shown any marked regionalist sympathies.

The Republicans were pledged to establish a consititutional democracy with a universally-elected parliament in the Cortes with far greater recognition of regionalist claims to equality, and representation. The conservative and commercial world suspected the motives of the republicans and distrusted their ability. So did the Church. Catholicism was the dominant religious force in the country. There were no signs of any willingness on the part of church leaders to modify their unrelenting hostility to any suggestion of liberalism. Even in 1936, to admit to voting liberal was to face excommunication.

The Church still retained great economic power and far-reaching organizational strength. Although the popular support for the liberal movement was a clear sign of an increasing resistance to its authority. This fact was even admitted by some churchmen. A Father Francisco Piero admitted, "In 1930, only five per cent of the Catholic population was attending mass. The figure in Madrid and other cities was as low as one per cent". But the Church was still able to create great pressure and became the centre of ideological resistance to the Republic and the main organizer of resistance to it.

The army's attitude was more uncertain. There was an inevitable conflict of loyalty for some as a result of the religious conflict. But there was also a significant trend among some non-Catholic officers who either totally rejected religion or were non-conformists. Some of these were members of the society of Freemasons, traditionally in nineteenth-century Europe, the hotbed of anti-catholicism. They belonged to the influential Grand Orient Lodge in Madrid. Throughout the period of the Republic an oddly-assorted collection of politically motivated senior officers used the Lodge as a means of forwarding their own careers in the hope that their political attitudes would aid their promotion. When it came to the crunch most of them rallied to the rebels even if, in the beginning, some gave the impression of wavering.

In 1931, however, the army on the whole lacked an effective national character. Its image was blurred and its loyalties divided; there were monarchists, hard-line fascists, ultra-imperialist colonial soldiers and ambitious opportunists. The army was affected by many of the similar religious and regional considerations that were also influencing and dividing the politicians.

The Republican leaders were wrapped up in consititution-making and high-minded reforms. The death penalty was abolished. The Church was disestablished and separated from the state and the powerful Catholic Society of Jesuits was banned. The Republic was dedicated to the ballot-box concept of democracy to the disadvantage of effective economic and social policies. Little attention was paid to the urgent need for genuine land reform and agricultural development. Everyone could vote. But the opponents of the regime relied on being able to manipulate the so-called *woman's vote* through the power of the priests to exploit church authority through the confession box.

The conflict between the state and the church was particularly marked in the field of education. It was estimated that over eighty per cent of the population was unable to read and write. The new educational policy required a huge expansion of services, teachers and buildings but when it came to the point facilities were lacking. Parents could not afford the money to pay for books and materials. The only vacancies available were in fee-paying schools. The Church operated a boycott after the ban on church schools. Nuns refused to conform to instructions issued by the Ministry for Public Instruction. It was thought that there were more than 30,000 nuns and over 200,000 monks involved. The boycott paralysed the educational system. The Republic was forced to climb down to the extent of recognizing the right of the church to keep its authority over religious education so long as the clergy, priests and nuns, conformed to the teaching instructions and schedules of the lay authority.

The Republican government was also determined to take the army in hand. It was to be reorganized and democratized. There was to be an end to *camarillas* and political intrigues. Manuel Azana, a high-minded liberal lawyer and one of the key founding fathers of the Republic, was the Minister responsible. There was no doubt of his motives as an ardent supporter of the League of Nations and the cause of world disarmament. He was determined to purge the army of men dedicated to imperial conquests and who scorned to hide their hostility to the Republic.

One of Azana's first actions was to order the closure of the Saragossa Military Academy. General Franco was ordered to dismiss his staff. Many of them were former Foreign Legion colleagues and comrades from the Spanish colonial wars in North Africa. They were retired out of hand and sent packing without regard to their ranks or records. But Franco was luckier. He was merely demoted with loss of seniority though he was stripped of his medals. He was left on the shelf without a job for over a year. Then he was ordered to take over the command of the infantry garrison at Corunna.

Below Manuel Azana (1880-1940) was one of the founders of the Republic. He was responsible for purging the army of men who were hostile to the Republic and closing the Saragossa Military Academy.

This army purge began another Republican crisis. It was closely tied to the obvious lack of confidence in the liberal government of the industrial workers. This was particularly evident in the northwest among the miners in the Asturias mountains and the engineers and fitters of the metal works and steel factories around Oviedo. From the beginning it had been clear that there was a notable lack of support for the republic from the trade unions and political left, in spite of its determined libertarian image. The trade unions had deep roots among the working people of the country. They had been legalized in Spain back in 1881, and the Socialist Party was founded even earlier in 1879.

Below Lack of confidence in the Government led to industrial unrest and strikes. This picture shows bank clerks on strike in Madrid.

In the early 1930s the Libertarians were very much at large. They had always been suspicious of the middle-class politicians who appeared to be running the republic. The anarchists in particular, rejected parliamentary government. They were more concerned with extending their influence among the land-hungry peasants and unskilled urban workers. The radical left was also doubtful about the government's ability or willingness, to meet the challenges facing the regime — especially from the right wing.

The supposed growth of the anarchists, coupled with considerable industrial unrest and strikes, became the excuse and justification, in 1932, for the first serious officers' plot, under General José Sanjurjo, to overthrow the Republic. But news of the conspiracy leaked out too early. The free-talking irresponsible conspirator-in-chief actually broke his own security when he was drunk the night before the coup was due to take place. General Sanjurjo blurted out details of what was going to happen to the girl with whom he was planning on spending the night in a Madrid brothel. She found an excuse to get away from him long enough to inform the security police. Within a matter of hours, the chief conspirators were picked up and dealt with very quietly and severely. Sanjurjo was stripped of all honours and sent into permanent exile in Portugal.

The after-effects of the Sanjurjo plot were far-reaching. All officers suspected of having any connection with the plot were arrested, and sentences were harsh. For some time the Officer Corps nursed deep resentments against those who managed to avoid suspicion and among these was General Franco.

In contrast to many of his former colleagues, the General looked almost sympathetic to the republic. He was even promoted. But just to make sure, he was transferred from the mainland and sent to Majorca, as the Captain-General of the Balearic Islands. Some years later, during the crisis months after the 1936 elections when the General was having an important interview with Manuel Azana, then the last President of the Republic, he referred back to the Sanjurjo affair. "I knew all about these plots," he told the President, "but I preferred to stand aside and let them fail through their own inertia." "So did we," said the President.

The powerful church opposition to the radical undercurrents of the Republic was leading directly to the formation of powerful fascist movements. The first to be founded was the party of Catholic Action, known

Below The Catholic Church was a powerful force of opposition to any radical ideas of the Republic. The picture shows the Gypsy Virgin from an Easter procession in Seville.

by the initials CEDA. It was led by Jesus Maria Gil Robles, a shrewd ambitious lawyer who advocated the introduction of a corporate state on the style of Benito Mussolini's fascist model in Italy. In contrast, Don Antonio Primo de Rivera, son of the former dictator, launched a rival fascist movement known as the Falange. The Falange was closer to the Hitler National Socialist model than the CEDA. Its programme also put greater emphasis on the problems of social justice and national revival.

When elections took place in 1933 in a rapidly deteriorating economic situation, the Gil Robles coalition with Conservatives and other discontented right-wing groups was victorious. It successfully exploited the alleged political inexperience of women who exercised their right to vote for the first time. All this took place at the time of international fascist expansion. Hitler came to power in Germany, ignored the Versailles Treaty, and marched into the demilitarized zone along the river Rhine, and then took over Austria. Italy invaded Ethiopia.

In Spain the CEDA's electoral successes had sinister implications for the future. Francisco Franco had again emerged as the bright star of the army. He got back his military seniority and was also promoted. He again registered another "first" by becoming the youngest ever Major-General in the Spanish army. Equally significant perhaps, General Franco also began to show a marked interest in the fascist movement led by Gil Robles. This could, of course, be partly explained by the role of Ramon Serrano-Suner, his brother-in-law. Suner had been to an Italian university and had returned an enthusiastic supporter of Mussolini's fascism. He had emerged as the energetic and ambitious secretary of the Gil Robles youth movement *Accion Popular*.

In 1934, however, Suner resigned to join the more

> "The Falange flew the red-black flag symbolizing blood and death in proud imitation of the Anarchists who had flown the flag long before the Falange movement was invented. Anarchists and Fascists were brothers under the skin and death was always the landscape they understood best." *Stanley Payne,* Franco's Spain.

Above General Franco (with the Army cap) with his brother-in-law Ramon Serrano-Suner (on Franco's right).

dynamic pro-Nazi Falange. Suner's influence on Franco was becoming increasingly evident. As the years went by the relationship between Franco and his brother-in-law was the subject of many jokes circulating throughout the country. On publicity and propaganda posters Franco was usually shown in half-length poses. Suner, so the joke went, had stolen his trousers. But in fact, in 1934, the Spanish crisis was slowly coming to a head. And at that stage of development, Francisco Franco seemed shrewdly positioned to play a crucial role in determining its outcome.

5. Trouble in the North

General Franco was back in the centre of the next storm that was to shake the Republic at the end of 1934. He was in Madrid at the time, having been recalled from Majorca where he had been working as acting technical adviser to the General Staff. It was a period of continuous confrontation between the left, the republicans and the new government of another prominent right wing politician Alexander Lerroux. Gil Robles was also a key minister in it.

The trouble came to a head in the north, where over forty thousand miners in the Asturias were on strike. They were supported by socialists, communists and anarchists. The left wing also banked on receiving support from the Basque movement which was then being harried by the central government. The Lerroux administration repeatedly refused to acknowledge the right of the regional assemblies, set up under the constitution, to legislate for matters of particular local importance.

The government sent General Franco and his old friend General Goded to put down the revolt. Franco made himself notorious throughout the anti-fascist world at the time, by calling on the negro troops from the colonial army in Africa. The Moors, as they were called, went into action against the miners. It was the first time they had been seen on the mainland since the Moorish occupation in the Middle Ages was ended by the legendary El Cid. Some time later Constancia de la Mora, the fervent Republican granddaughter of the Marqués de Maura, a former Royalist Prime Minister,

Above In 1934 General Franco called in Moorish troops to put down the revolt in the Asturias. 40,000 miners went on strike and over 1,000 people were killed in the revolt.

wrote in her diary of "the hated General Franco who sent the Moors to rape and kill in the Asturias".

Over a thousand people were killed in the Asturias revolt. Thousands more were jailed, interrogated, and tortured. A parliamentary commission appointed by the Cortes to investigate reports of brutality against the prisoners confirmed many of the most unpleasant allegations. General Franco was still there, even when the fog cleared a little. Although officially he had been given a new appointment as Commander of the Legion in Morocco, Gil Robles, now War Minister, had kept him at his side as an official adviser.

But the Government was under attack and rocking. There were serious allegations being made of political and financial corruption. Prime Minister Lerroux was implicated, as was one of the main financial backers of the Falange, the industrialist Juan March.

On 17th May, 1935, Gil Robles formally appointed Franco as Chief of Staff. The War Minister approved of Franco's determination to reverse the democratization of the army intended by the founding fathers of the Republic. The General was clearly determined to re-instate many of the officers who had been cashiered and disgraced for anti-Republican actions. One of his first actions was to give Emilio Mola, now a General, a new command, in Morocco. He also promoted one of Sanjurjo's aides, Colonel Varela, to the rank of General. The future fascist generals, Yague and Orgaz, were also promoted and given important jobs at the War Office. Franco smartened things up. He insisted on proper work routines and greater efficiency. He even set a personal example by always arriving at the office before 9 a.m.

But more significant was the recommissioning and re-appointment of some eighty officers, previously disciplined by liberal Republicans. They all received notice of their re-instatement from President Alcala Zamora, a liberal who had remained Head of the Republic throughout the changes of government. The President complained bitterly to the War Minister that only four of the officers had had the decency to acknowledge his willingness to restore them to their places in the army. But Gil Robles, who treated the President as a mere figure-head replied cynically: "Presumably they were not aware of protocol".

> "We must move towards a new state. What matters if it means shedding blood." *Gil Robles, 1934.*

6. Popular Front

A far-reaching reaction against the fascist threat to liberty was setting in in Europe around 1935. It was closely related to the certainty of millions of people of the obvious drive to war of the German and Italian fascist leaders—Hitler and Mussolini. In Britain eleven million people took part in what was known as "the Peace Ballot" organized by the League of Nations Union. It was, essentially, an anti-fascist demonstration.

In France, liberals, radicals, and activists of all parties were increasingly concerned at the growth and spread of fascist ideas and they formed a widely-based anti-fascist movement. A French electoral alliance of radical-socialist liberals, socialists and communists came into existence in 1935. It swept the country as the "popular front" and a new Popular Front government was formed in France under the socialist leader, Leon Blum in 1936.

A similar electoral alliance came into existence among the Spanish Republicans. It was also known as the *frente popular* (Popular Front). On 16th February, 1936, it swept to power by winning 271 out of the 473 seats in the Cortés. The rival "National Front", the alliance of the reactionary and fascist movements, only got 132 seats. The National Front included the right wing conservative and clerical parties as well as the fascists, and several different brands of monarchists.

The so-called National Front was committed to the introduction of a corporate state on the lines of what

Opposite page Hitler and Mussolini, the two fascist leaders of Europe, pictured together before the outbreak of World War Two.

Below Leon Blum, the French socialist leader who headed the electoral alliance of political parties known as the "Popular Front".

had happened in Germany and Italy. The Popular Front programme, on the other hand, aimed to maintain and strengthen the 1931 Liberal constitution. To some outsiders, however, it looked as though the liberals, the regional groups and the socialists were working with the trade unions and the extreme left to impose a new revolutionary regime.

The Popular Front government was under strong pressure to introduce its full programme immediately, particularly in such areas as land reform, industrial expansion and improvement in the working conditions and wages of the notoriously badly paid Spanish workers.

By April, some of the huge estates belonging to absentee landlords were being taken over and worked by the peasants themselves. Parliament went half-way towards ordering the redistribution of estates, particularly in the south, but land hungry *braceros* took the matter even further. There was a virtually continuous outbreak of strikes and industrial unrest coupled with increasingly violent clashes between the partisans and strong-arm thugs of the respective rival political groups. The hostile and bitter critics of the regime in the army were rapidly approaching the point of no return.

Secret moves were being made. The Republic was to be brought down. The trade union movement and the left-wing political parties, socialists, communists and anarchists, were to be suppressed; so were the liberals if they did not accept the situation. Some army leaders were ready to bring fascism to Spain. They had been thinking along the lines of the Italian model rather than the German. But they had already been in contact with the leaders of both countries and were confident that they could rely on Italy and Germany for active military, economic and material aid as well as diplomatic support.

Plans were afoot to establish a military committee of senior army commanders to take over and establish a new fascist state. This *junta* was to be headed by the exiled veteran General Sanjurjo. Franco, at that stage, did not figure among the active leaders of the conspiracy. But it is difficult to believe that he was unaware of what was happening. All the indications are that he knew of every move that was being made.

The previous October, when he was Chief of Staff, he had been directly approached about the possibility of the army taking over in order to forestall Popular Front moves to replace the discredited Lerroux administration. Gil Robles, still Minister of War under Lerroux, had personally sounded out Franco about the possibility of an army move to block the elections that would inevitably follow the collapse of the Lerroux government.

Franco had warned Robles against acting too hastily. He did not believe that all the possibilities for finding a political solution had yet been exhausted. He was hoping for political moves to break the Popular Front alliance by isolating the left wing. There were also doubts whether the army had sufficient political unity to carry out a successful *coup d'état.*

General Franco was clearly lurking in the shadows of the political centre. On the night of the declaration of the results of the February election, a few months later, he was actually meeting the disgruntled leaders of the opposition to the Republic. At a secret meeting in Madrid the General was pressed to exploit his position as the strong-man who had suppressed the 1934 Asturias troubles. They wanted him to intervene personally and declare martial law. But Francisco Franco was not yet ready to move. Once again he held his hand and advised his supporters to be patient.

The following month there was another approach of even greater urgency. The General was again pressed

to take immediate action against the Popular Front
government. But Franco remained firm. He insisted
that action was still premature, though his next moves
indicated that he was banking on divisions within the
Government reaching a point when the moderates
would break away and call for his help to outlaw the
left wing groups as a threat to the security of the state.

The developing crisis of the new government was
also evident in the Cortes, where the old President
Zamora had been forced out in a constitutional
argument over his authority. His place was taken by
Manuel Azana, the former Minister for the Army, who
had once dismissed Franco as the commandant of the
Saragossa Military Academy. Now he was determined
to put as big a distance as possible between the
dangerous General and his friends by sending him to
virtual exile in the Canary Islands.

The order instructing Franco to report to the Canary
Islands as Captain General was immediately used by
the General as the excuse to pressurize President Azana
with a scarcely veiled threat. Franco immediately asked
for a personal interview with Azana at which he pressed
the President to seek Government reconsideration of
the order to transport him to the Canaries. "I can be of
much more use to Spain where I am", he said to the
President.

In the light of what was afoot, General Franco's
remark was, again, a considerable understatement.
The crafty General Mola was already hard at work
undermining the Republic from his headquarters as
the garrison commander of the important religious
centre and capital of Navarre, Burgos. He was laying
the ground-work for a military rising. As the former
Director of Army Intelligence during the last days of
the monarchy, he was in a position to bring together
the various strands of opposition to the Republic in the
army. He had already established an effective courier

42

and communications system. Mola was also able to rely on important political contacts to establish diplomatic and international support, as well as arrange for military supplies and equipment and also personnel to come from fascist Italy and Nazi Germany. The figure-head of the conspiracy was to be General Sanjurjo.

In April 1936 the draft of a proclamation to accompany the setting up of a military *junta* was being circulated. But it was withdrawn as premature. General Franco, in the wings, was still not willing to commit himself to such a compromising move.

The future Caudillo was even prepared, once more, to drop another broad hint to the President of the extent of the opposition it was about to encounter. On 25th June, 1936, General Franco actually sent President Azana a "final warning". Was he hoping at that late hour to be called back to Madrid and installed, constitutionally, as the strong-man to save Spain both from the left and the right? Whatever the reason behind Franco's action, the President again snubbed the General. President Azana remained loyal to the Republic to the end. But the General had also reached the point of no return, and from then on committed himself to the military revolt, and the absolute destruction of the Spanish Republic and the Popular Front.

Below General Franco (nearer the camera) with General Mola embracing on the balcony of the rebel headquarters in Burgos.

7. Generals in Revolt

The "Lion of the Riffs", General Sanjurjo, was the recognized leader of the conspiracy. During his exile he had been working to exploit his international reputation. He was not, in world terms, a big man, and was therefore able to travel around the capitals of Europe without drawing attention to himself. He had visited both Rome and Berlin where he had been given due honours.

Both Hitler and Mussolini had received Sanjurjo. Their willingness to meet him personally implied more than just courtesy. It was tacit approval of the alleged "civilizing mission" of serving officers in the Spanish army dedicated to the forcible overthrow of the Republic. It was, after all, consistent with their own attitudes, for they were still seeking to secure in their own countries fascist regimes of similar brutality to that being prepared for Spain.

Sanjurjo had obtained firm promises of support and aid in terms of munitions, supplies—and men. Spanish grandees and absentee landlords, as well as high churchmen and catholic politicians, had also been canvassing international support for a regime in Spain, but more in line with Spanish traditions and customs. They also relied on the backing and support of two well-known men of affairs with large financial and commercial interests.

The names of Francisco Cambo and Juan March were synonymous with high finance and international big business. They both had important links with the City of London, international banking and, in particular, the Rio Tinto mining corporation. Rio Tinto had a world reputation as a company operating in Spain almost entirely on international capital supplied by foreign investors. The support of such men as Cambo and March clearly contained implicit assurances to those prepared to back the Spanish conspirators, that their investment, no matter what form it took, would duly pay handsome dividends at some future date.

While Sanjurjo and his fellow-travellers were hawking their cause around the Chancelleries of Europe, General Mola had shifted the centre of his spider's web to Pamplona, another important northern garrison town and religious centre. Other key figures of the conspiracy were also busy. Queipo de Llano, the

Left General Sanjurjo, known as the "Lion of the Riffs".

Above General Queipo de Llano, who used his influence to gather support for the rebels.

bushy-browed Inspector-General of Carabineros, was speeding through the countryside in his huge official Hispano-Suza car. He visited garrison towns and seaports making contacts, twisting the arms of uncertain supporters and recruiting others. He was a member of the Grand Orient Masonic Lodge and used his masonic influence to some effect. Later, he boasted that he had travelled over twelve thousand miles on behalf of the conspiracy at official government expense.

An important group of middle-rank officers had been made responsible for checking on the actions and behaviour of suspicious persons. They were in a position to exercise influence at the right place when the time came. Later, numerous incidents were reported of reluctant rebel commanders having guns shoved in the small of their necks and given ten seconds to choose. In most cases, it seems, they needed even less time to amend their principles.

There was no doubt where the decisive element of the revolt was to be found. It came from the hard-core of tough Old Guard warriors of the Foreign Legion. All of them were close companions-in-arms of Francisco Franco. None of them had any doubt that when the time came he would throw the whole of his weight and prestige behind them. Franco had already sent Mola a cryptic, but significant, message. "When the time comes", he wrote, "I will do my duty."

Franco's hesitancy, however, was clearly not to the liking of the impatient General Sanjurjo. He was annoyed at the delays and frustrations of the conspirators, in his hideaway in Portugal. The hot-tempered old man had no reason to sympathize with Franco's doubts and uncertainties. He was not likely to forget the role Franco had played in 1932. Sanjurjo was convinced that Franco, then, had let him down. Was he going to do it again? Sanjurjo made no attempt to hide his attitude when the time for action arrived. "With or without Franquito, we go ahead!" he ordered Major José Antonio Ansaldo, the young pilot who had been sent to bring "The Lion" back to Spain as soon as the revolt was declared.

Ansaldo had arrived at Estoril in an Italian plane. He had actually piloted it back from Rome only a few days earlier. He had first stopped off at Pamplona to see Mola. His instructions were to fly directly to Estoril, pick up Sanjurjo and fly back to Madrid. Sanjurjo, he found, was in no mood for delays. But there were some hold-ups before Ansaldo's aircraft was cleared for the return journey. The Portuguese government, in spite of the fascist nature of the regime, had not been able to ignore the diplomatic protest it had already received from the Spanish Republican government in Madrid, for allowing General Sanjurjo to intrigue with the army rebels. The Republic claimed that it amounted to interference in the internal affairs of Spain. The presence of the rebel aircraft on an official Portuguese military base was cause for further concern. Ansaldo had been told to shift his aircraft as fast as possible, although President Salazar of Portugal had allowed him to land at a small civilian airstrip nearer the General's villa at La Marinha. The General was waiting impatiently, together with his luggage: two suitcases crammed to bursting with the official regalia and uniforms for a future fascist president.

Ansaldo warned the General that the aircraft was already overloaded with extra fuel needed for the journey. He urged Sanjurjo to leave the bags to be sent on later. But the old man absolutely refused. How could the Head of State of the new fascist Spain be expected to preside over the victory parade anticipated in Madrid in the next few days, if he was not properly dressed?

Ansaldo, apparently, was unable to insist on the

General conforming to his request. The aircraft took off badly overloaded and crashed. At least, that is the way Ansaldo tells it in his autobiography—*The Memoirs of a Spanish Monarchist.* In describing what happened he wrote: "A moment before the plane was due to take off into the air I heard a violent knocking sound and this was followed by a sudden shaking of the whole plane. I thought, perhaps, a wheel had smashed but pulled the stick back. I had the feeling that even with a broken wheel it would still be possible to make a landing.

"However, as we flew over the trees I realized that our speed was becoming progressively slower, instead of increasing. There was a danger the airplane might break up while in flight. The shaking was also growing worse. It occurred to me that the propeller might have broken. We were no longer at the speed necessary to maintain flight so I decided to come down. I cut off the motor and aimed for a ploughed field directly in front of me. Between the ground and the airplane there was a wall about three feet high. Somehow I had to get the plane over the wall. The heat and the weight of the heavily-loaded plane prevented it and we crashed on top of the wall. If there had been only two or three inches of leeway we should have got over it safely and somehow brought the plane to the ground without much harm being done.

"At this moment sensation and memories were all mixed-up . . . I seemed to be half-conscious like someone waking from a deep and pleasant sleep. I knew I was covered with blood but felt no pain. The General was sitting there but his face seemed oddly sprinkled with white powder. . . . The airplane was in flames. I tried to open the cockpit but the door was locked. My wrist was broken. I shouted to the General. We were on fire but he made no move. His lips were half-open and smiling. My uniform was burning.

Mechanically, without knowing what I was doing I somehow succeeded in opening the door. . . ." Ansaldo lost consciousness. When he came to he was on the ground but the General was still inside smiling as the flames mounted. By the time help arrived the wreck was a blazing inferno. The General was not only dead; he had been cremated—with his uniforms.

In contrast, General Franco was in a far better position. In spite of Sanjurjo's sharp dismissal of "Franquito", Francisco Franco had not missed his chance. While the luckless Sanjurjo was being burned he had only got his feet wet. He was already airborne. His moment of truth had arrived. He was in the de Haviland aircraft hired in London by his influential friend, and piloted by a former officer in the British airforce. He was on his way. A new leader was ready to take the centre of the Spanish stage.

Below Following the death of General Sanjurjo, Franco was poised to take over the leadership of the rebellion. Here he watches the advance of his troops on the Catalonian front during the civil war.

8. International Illusions

After 18th July, 1936, there were few signs of Franco dragging his feet. The steps he was taking confirmed the worst suspicions of those who had hesitated to trust him. They were also evidence of his political shrewdness if not, directly, of his ruthlessness. The disappearance from the scene of the man who would clearly have out-ranked him in the hierarchy of the Generals' *junta* was, perhaps, more than a mere coincidence.

Franco was clearly gathering authority into his own hands. He had already issued a manifesto of his own calling on Spaniards to rise against the alleged "red menace" of the Popular Front. He had called for, and obtained, the allegiance of the colonial "Army of Africa" which had seized control of Morocco. But everything was not going as well for them as it was for Franco. The position on the mainland was far less decisive. The attempt of the commanding generals to seize power in most of the major garrison towns of the Republic was meeting fierce and spontaneous resistance.

Barricades were going up everywhere throughout Spain. The partisans of the Popular Front were forming themselves into a Peoples' Antifascist Militia. Paving stones, cobbles, bricks and scaffolding were ripped up; cars were overturned; taxis, buses and trucks were seized to transport the militia reinforcements to hard-pressed areas. Everyone seemed to be joining in. The trade unions had called for a complete stoppage of work. Workers in blue dungarees and overalls were joined by peasants from outlying areas, shopkeepers, waiters, taxidrivers, boot-blacks, beggars, and even prostitutes. Army conscripts were being forced into action by rebel officers and ordered to seize important buildings, telephone exchanges, government offices and town-halls. Many deserted to join the militia. In some towns the fighting was so fierce that blood ran in the gutters. The bodies of horses killed in the fighting were dragged into public squares and burned.

The peoples' militia had powerful mass support, boundless energy and initiative. But it was short of arms, equipment and ammunition. Old blunderbusses, flintlocks and ancient muskets supplemented rusty swords, pikes and farm implements. In the country areas peasants reacted as sharply as the town republicans when soldiers or civil guards attempted to seize town-halls or close meeting places. Those who showed any inclination to side with the rebels or protect the property of the great landlords were set upon and often slaughtered. Town Halls were taken over by the militia. Popular Front committees began to introduce a new social order as resistance to the generals mounted among the common people throughout Spain.

There were huge popular demonstrations in Madrid, Barcelona, Bilbao, Malaga and other key centres. The clergy were seen to be hand-in-glove with the military. Churches were frequently attacked and destroyed. They were suspected of being refuges for fascist snipers or hidden arms depots. There were continuous wild rumours of spies and snipers in bell-towers and vestries. In the capital city, Madrid, after a particularly tense and violent struggle to reduce the main rebel strongholds, there was a continuous demonstration outside the Cortes calling on the government to order the general distribution of arms and weapons to the

> "Thousands of trade unionists, employed and unemployed, irrespective of age, dock workers, labourers, shop assistants, office clerks were flocking to recruiting depots for the militia. Brigades were being assembled in former army barracks found in the different quarters of the city. There was no sex discrimination. Girls were as welcome as boys. Everyone was in a high state of elation and euphoria after the victory of the streets. They were being packed into trucks and wagons and rushed off to the fronts being formed outside important centres of resistance...."
> *Richard Kisch,* They Shall Not Pass.

> "Caesar's commentaries on Spain tell us more than newspaper reports. The Spaniards fought with a violence which terrified Caesar, who on one famous occasion panicked in their midst. Throughout history, the Spanish have fought with relentless passion to annihilate and subdue their enemies." *Stanley Payne,* Franco's Spain.

Above One of the many huge demonstrations held throughout major Spanish cities before the outbreak of the civil war.

people. It lasted several days. The liberal politicians in the central government were forced to concede. The Prime Minister, Casares Quiroga, a liberal of no outstanding significance—except that he came from Galicia, the same province as Franco—dithered until he was replaced by another political nonentity, José Giral, a former university chemistry professor. Giral at least gave instructions for arms to be distributed to the militia through the trade unions.

The rebels increasingly found themselves facing an enraged population-in-arms. In many places they were forced to surrender or retreat to the strongholds they had succeeded in securing. Most of the professional army and airforce supported them. But the Navy did not. Sailors loyal to the Republic had seized most of the Spanish fleet. It was hoped that ships of the Navy could be used to blockade the North African coast and prevent Franco from sending reinforcements to the mainland. It looked like deadlock. The rebels' hopes of a 24-hour walk-over had been frustrated. It took them almost three years before they finally succeeded.

At the end of July 1936, the rebels controlled only a thick strip of land in the north, stretching from the Pyrenees frontier in Navarre, south and west to the Portuguese frontier and the Atlantic coast below Bilbao. But the important Asturias industrial and

Below A map showing the progress of the Spanish Civil War.

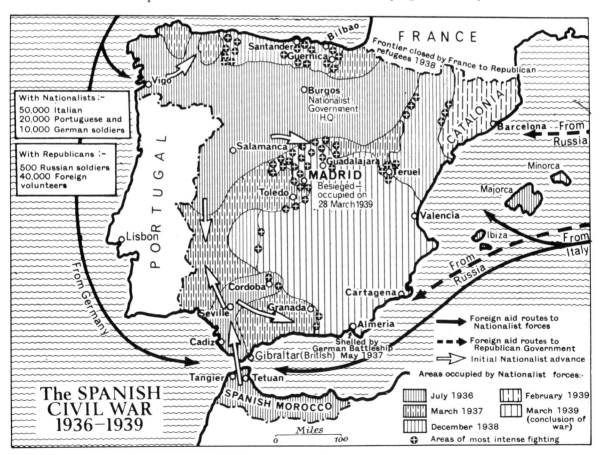

With Nationalists :-
50,000 Italian
20,000 Portuguese and
10,000 German soldiers

With Republicans :-
500 Russian soldiers
40,000 Foreign volunteers

FRANCE

Frontier closed by France to Republican refugees 1938

CATALONIA

Barcelona --From Russia

Minorca

Majorca

From Italy

Ibiza

From Russia

Valencia

Cartagena

Almeria

Santander
Guernica
Bilbao
Vigo
Burgos
Nationalist Government H.Q.
Salamanca
Guadalajara
Teruel
MADRID
Besieged — occupied on 28 March 1939
Toledo

PORTUGAL

Lisbon

Cordoba
Granada
Seville
Cadiz
Shelled by German Battleship Gibraltar (British) May 1937
Tangier
Tetuan
SPANISH MOROCCO

From Germany

The SPANISH CIVIL WAR 1936-1939

→ Foreign aid routes to Nationalist forces
⇢ Foreign aid routes to Republican Government
⇨ Initial Nationalist advance

Areas occupied by Nationalist forces:-

July 1936   February 1939
March 1937   March 1939 (conclusion of war)
December 1938
✛ Areas of most intense fighting

Miles
0   100

mining complex was Republican. There was also another crucial stronghold in the south-west around Seville. This was almost the personal possession of General Queipo de Llano. He had not only seized Seville virtually single-handed but had, at the same time, established and consolidated a vital bridgehead on the mainland for the black moorish troops that General Franco was to bring over to the mainland from North Africa. Queipo de Llano also took personal charge of the Seville Radio, and from then on until the end of the war, was notorious for the stream of abuse and obscenities that he poured out against the Republic over the air.

The fate of the revolt against the Republic had been left almost entirely in the hands of General Francisco Franco. He alone among the rebel generals controlled sufficient troops in the Army of Africa; but, even more important, he also possessed the political shrewdness to unite the rebel generals into a cohesive force and later, after establishing his personal power, to balance and control the new system he was establishing. General Franco also achieved something else. He effectively raised the whole basis of the rebel operation to a new level, by converting a civil war into an international war scare. He was counting on receiving substantial military aid from fascist Italy and Nazi Germany. He organized the first military airlift in history by using German Dornier and Junker transport planes to fly ten thousand moorish troops and four thousand members of the Spanish Foreign Legion from Ceuta in Morocco to Jerez, on the mainland.

The actual intervention of German and Italian troops on Franco's side helped to foster illusions calculated to disarm rather than to alert European politicians to the real threat to themselves of fascism, particularly Nazism under Hitler. The German *führer* had already shown himself a past-master of exploiting

fears of Soviet Russia by claiming to be *"the bulwark against Bolshevism"*. Now Franco was taking a page out of his master's book by acting as though he had a divine mission to save Spain (and by implication the rest of Christian Europe) from Soviet communism. The situation was designed to encourage fears, particularly in British and French financial and political circles, that the Spanish Republic was being taken over by international communists. An international war scare was blown up. So-called experts, the men in the Foreign Offices, came up with a suggestion to cool things down. The idea was to put the Spanish Republic into quarantine, and that countries should be ordered not to intervene in Spanish affairs. The proposal came

Above During the Spanish Civil War Hitler sent German soldiers and arms to help Franco's army. Because of Germany's involvement, an international war scare developed.

too late to prevent Germany and Italy from sending troops, supplies and aircraft, but it put the Spanish Government in great difficulties. The Republic was being cut off from its vital traditional sources of supply, particularly from France. It was slowly being squeezed to death. The effect of "non-intervention" in practice was to blockade the Spanish Republic but not the fascists. Dr Juan Negrin, the last Prime Minister of the Republic, a socialist, bitterly described the situation at the last meeting of the Republican Cortes, in the northern town of Figueras, on 1st February, 1939. It was a little more than a month before the final death of the Republic. "Our terrible and tremendous problem", said Negrin, "has always been lack of arms. We are a legitimate government and we have had to resort to buying arms clandestinely as contraband, even in Germany and Italy."

The Republic had only one consistent, open supporter. Up to the end it managed to obtain limited supplies and assistance from the USSR, in the form of solidarity. But there were some obvious reasons why the Soviet Union (then the only socialist state in the world) would not have been over-anxious to expose itself to retaliation from its chief fascist enemies. By offering a direct challenge in a strategic area it would have been put at a disadvantage, in view of the relative geographical positions of Spain and the USSR. The Russians, however, did send expert military advisers to assist the Republican army, as well as aircraft and some heavy guns and tanks.

The other source of aid from which the Republic benefited was the concern of many ordinary people at what was happening in the name of "Non-Intervention". Within a matter of months from the establishment of the twenty-two-nation Non-Intervention Committee a stream of volunteers from all over the world had made their way to Spain, to fight with the Republican army in what became known as the International Brigade. By 1939, thirty thousand volunteers had passed through this famous corps.

The other side of the "balance-sheet" of Non-Intervention showed just what a nonsense it had become by the end of the war in March 1939. Neither Germany nor Italy had attempted to disguise the aid they had been sending to Franco. There were over thirty thousand German panzer troops in the Nazi Condor Legion. It was equipped with ultra-modern German fighter planes, as well as bombers and tanks. The German pilots who were to become the Luftwaffe ace fliers of World War Two began their careers in Spain. They were also able to try out experimental fighting techniques as well as hideous terror-bombing. The destruction of the world-famous Basque holy town of Guernica by German bombers was the forerunner of the pattern-bombing used by the Luftwaffe to destroy Coventry and other British cities during World War Two. Franco and his colleagues did not try to prevent Spanish soil from being used for battle-practice for the coming war. Even the famous German aircraft manufacturer and designer Willy Messerschmitt paid a special visit to Spain himself to test out advanced fighter plane designs which were to be the future Second World War aircraft.

German battleships patrolled Spanish waters with the blockade patrols of the Non-Intervention Committee. The *Leipzig* even lobbed shells into the middle of the naval port of Almeria held by the Republicans. The pocket battleships *Graf von Spee*, *Tirpitz* and *Deutschland* also took part in the patrols. Bruno Mussolini, son of the Italian leader was among the 50,000 Italian blackshirts in Spain. The Italian fascists were hoping to extend their power bases in the Mediterranean and hoped to retain the airbases they had seized for their own in Majorca and the other

"The landlords were attempting to stage a boycott in order to crush the labourers. Any work they gave had to be forced out of them. If we had let them be, every vineyard in Mijas, every single vine would have been abandoned—as indeed happened when the nationalists entered. Then the landlords rooted out all their vines. Of all the vines which produced the raisins the town used to export, only the two poorest are left." *Manuel Cortés, former Mayor of Mijas, in conversation with Ronald Fraser, In Hiding.*

Above The shattered ruins of the Basque town of Guernica, bombed flat by the German Luftwaffe during the Spanish Civil War.

Balearic Islands. Portugal's fascist leader, Salazar, had also provided Franco with military support in the shape of 20,000 conscripts.

The Spanish civil war lasted almost three years, from July 1936 until March 1939. During that time General Franco and his supporters carved up the Spanish Republic and destroyed its democratic institutions. Hundreds of thousands of lives were lost through the use of torture and repressions, second only to those introduced by the German Nazis.

General Franco became an international figure almost rivalling Hitler and Mussolini in the arrogance of his attitudes and the ruthlessness of his personal authority. After the death of General Sanjurjo Franco steadily strengthened his power and control over the so-called Spanish nationalists. He went from being, initially, just "one among equals" in his relationships to his fellow conspirators to being the all-powerful General Franco. His personal role in the direction of the rebel war effort does not seem to have been particularly outstanding, but it was evident that potential alternative leaders conveniently disappeared before challenges developed. Franco also successfully re-organized and secured the national fascist movement known as the Falange very much as a personal instrument to consolidate his position. Much later, however, he found it convenient to switch positions and return to his earlier monarchist commitment. But the Caudillo's progress to one-man rule was not achieved without occasional displays of his ability and determination to play the part of Spain's Man of Destiny.

Below Victims of the civil war. Hundreds of thousands of people were killed, and for almost three years Spanish streets ran with blood.

9. The Road to Power

When the rebellion began General Franco seemed almost a reluctant hero. There was no clear indication that within three months he would emerge as Supreme Commander and the designated Head of State of a new fascist regime. His path was cleared by a series of accidents which removed officers of possibly greater seniority from the field of challenge.

The first to go had been José Sanjurjo. The mystery of his puzzling death has never been fully cleared up, in spite of later post-war investigation. Sanjurjo's death was followed almost immediately by the loss to the fascists of General Franco's close comrade-in-arms, General Manuel Goded. The aristocratic Goded had shared the command with Franco when, in October 1934, they had been instructed to put down the strike of miners in the Asturias mountains. At the time of the Generals' Plot, General Goded was Captain-General of the Balearic Islands. He was well positioned to fly from his headquarters at Majorca to take over in Barcelona if the revolt had gone according to plan. But unfortunately for Goded his intelligence staff seem to have been misinformed about the reality of the situation in Barcelona. The General walked into a trap. He had flown to the airport by the harbour expecting to move into the nearby Governor's palace, only to find himself surrounded by militia-men and captured. Although Goded was immediately put under the personal protection of the Liberal President of Catalonia, Luis Companys, he was tried for treason to

Below The trial of two rebel leaders, Goded (left) and Burriel. They were found guilty, sentenced to death and shot on the morning of 12th August, 1936.

the Republic and executed. Could General Franco possibly have been aware of the advantages that might come to him from the death of his old friend?

Then came the loss of *el Director,* General Emilio Mola. The chief organizer of the military conspiracy was also killed in an aircrash. Was it coincidence? Mola had been flying to the central front to take command of the fascist forces again converging on Madrid in June 1937. Franco was curiously abrupt and almost cynical when he heard of Mola's death. "Replaceable in wartime: indispensable in peace. He will be sadly missed," he said. Franco's comment seems not only ungenerous but inappropriate, since at that time General Mola was conspicuously the only fascist commander to have made any territorial gain. His forces, largely black African moors, had re-occupied most of north-west Spain, including the Basque country. Don Antonio Primo de Rivera, likely to have emerged as the chief civilian rival to Franco, if he had survived, had also conveniently been removed from the Spanish scene. He had been arrested by Republican security forces almost immediately after the revolt was declared. He was charged with treason to the Republic. The accusation maintained that he was not only with the conspirators before the revolt was launched, but also had remained in contact with them even after his arrest. Don Antonio, son of the former dictator and founder of the Falange movement, was probably the only civilian fascist leader who might have been able to challenge Franco as the future popular leader of the country.

Several other potential challengers to Franco made their positions clear during the early struggles for power in the months following the July revolt of 1936. They drew attention to themselves by making keynote speeches at patriotic parades and functions. They seemed a singularly unattractive group of men with a

Above The last picture taken of General Mola, second in command to General Franco. He was killed in an air crash on 3rd June, 1937.

"I am not one of those who say they despise life when they are in a situation like mine. Life is not a firework one lets off at a garden party." *Don Antonio Primo de Rivera. Plea against death sentence after trial by Republican authorities for high treason, November 1935, Alicante.*

notable lack of political ability and a devastating weakness for dividing rather than uniting the miscellaneous social forces behind the rebellion.

General Queipo de Llano was one of the first openly to question Franco's right to assume the leadership of the revolt. The confrontation occurred in October 1936, shortly before the decisive meeting of the *junta* at Burgos, at which Franco's leadership role was confirmed. Queipo de Llano not only kept Franco waiting when he arrived for a "patriotic fiesta" at Seville, but had plastered the walls of the city with pictures of himself instead of the official posters bearing the head of Franco. However, he made a speech of such incredible stupidity that there was never any serious chance of his challenge developing after it, and he retired bruised. He was never even offered a government job in the years to come.

Even more important was a clash at Salamanca. The war-scarred veteran commander of the Tercio Corps, Millan Astray, tried to take on in debate Spain's greatest sage, the philosopher Miguel de Unamuno, the respected Rector of the University. It was a great occasion for dons and academicians dressed in their gaudy flowing robes and befurred capes, and also fashionably dressed socialites and the church leaders. Franco was not there, but his wife Dona Carmen sat next to the Rector. Astray, flanked by blue-shirted Falange storm-troopers, plunged into the attack with his battle-cry "Down with Intelligence! Long live death!"

The philosopher's contempt was withering. He concluded the debate: "You may win but you will not convince. You will win because you possess more than enough brute force, but you will not convince because to convince means to persuade. And in order to persuade you would need what you lack—reason and right in the struggle. I consider it futile to exhort you to

62

think of Spain. I have finished." Astray wanted Unamuno executed. So did some of the others. Instead Franco commuted the sentence to perpetual house arrest. But the philosopher had a brain haemorrhage and died on 31st December, 1936.

The declaration that put General Franco into the unique position of supreme commander and head of the so-called Nationalist state was made on 1st October, 1936. The initiative was taken by the airforce commander, General Kindelan. A special meeting of the *junta* was called at Burgos in the last week of September to appoint a supreme commander. The

Below General Franco taking the oath during the ceremony proclaiming him Supreme Head of the Nationalist Government.

question of whether to establish a nationalist government was also under discussion. Nobody objected when Kindelan put Franco's name forward as Commander-in-Chief of the Nationalist forces. But it was a different matter when it came to the question of government. General Miguel Cabanellas, formerly regarded as a strong Republican, objected. So did Queipo. Both of them were Masons. Mola was also in opposition. Cabanellas became the man in the middle. He was appointed President of the *junta* after voting firmly against a proposition that the job of Supremo and Head of the Government be doubled by the same person.

The announcement of General Franco's position as supreme commander was held up for a week while members of the *junta* prepared for a decisive confrontation which would hold back the monarchists and other opposition groups without definitely blocking the establishment of a definite dictatorship. A dramatic session of the *junta* had been attended by Franco, flanked by Kindelan and Yague, a future general and a key figure from the Legion. Kindelan produced a draft document nominating Franco as head of a fully-fledged fascist government under a national dictator. Yague had threatened a revolt of shock troops if the ultimatum was rejected. The other generals were faced with a bloodless *fait accompli* which was subject to nominal modification only for the sake of appearances.

When the formal proclamation was made on 1st October, General Franco was confirmed as supreme commander and "chief of state". The Caudillo was now ready and willing for the job. There was no sign of any change of opinion. Nor was there any let-up in the ruthless retaliation authorized by the Caudillo as the fascists gradually secured complete control over Spain after the surrender of the Republic in 1939.

10. Tightrope Walker

Generalissimo Franco issued the last communiqué of the Spanish war on 18th May, 1939. He had a nasty virus infection at the time, but there were far more headaches to come. After nearly three years of civil war Spain was in a precarious state. The economy was shattered; the social organization was in shreds. Some fifteen per cent of the national wealth had been destroyed and many towns were completely in ruins. The country's livestock had been slaughtered in enormous numbers. The jails were full and executions and torture were a way of life. The financial cost of the war had been astronomical and Spain was deeply in debt.

When the Second World War started a few months later, in September 1939, the Caudillo had to walk with extreme caution. He was on a tightrope. Franco's allies, Germany and Italy, were pressing hard for the payment of war debts, for equipment and material. They expected to receive it in kind, or in strategic advantage. The Mussolini regime came off worst. The Italian fascists received little cash to pay the wages of their troops in Spain, the so-called *Corpo di Truppo Voluntarier.* But the Duce hoped to strengthen Italian sea power at the western end of the Mediterranean by holding onto the Balearic Islands. He did not expect British counter-pressure. A Royal Navy destroyer, the *Devonshire,* was conveniently on hand to enable Franco to establish a Spanish governor at Palma de Majorca during the concluding stages of the war. After that Mussolini seemed to give up hope of getting back his loans.

The Nazis were more sophisticated and successful— at least to the extent of getting important raw materials for war production. They had set up, even during the civil war, joint Hispano-German trading, exporting and development companies. A certain Johannes Burkhardt ran the commercial side of the organization which was directed by Admiral Canaris, head of the German intelligence system. German mining operations were going ahead in Morocco. The Nazis were also hoping to grab important interests such as Rio Tinto, in which British investors had considerable influence. But German economic infiltration was blocked by Franco's decree against overseas financial interests obtaining more than 49 per cent holdings in Spanish concerns. The Nazis then tried diplomacy. They also wanted Nationalist Spain to commit itself unreservedly to the Nazi "New Order".

A personal meeting between Adolf Hitler and Francisco Franco was not a success. It took place on 12th October, 1940. Franco started by keeping Hitler waiting. He had arrived at San Sebastian on one side of the frontier while Hitler was waiting at Hendaye on the other. The journey between the towns normally takes half-an-hour. It took Franco three hours. Hitler clearly found Franco evasive and irritating and got less than he wanted from the meeting. "I'd rather have two teeth pulled out than meet that man again," he is reported to have said later.

Franco maintained his opposition to permanent German bases in Spain. But he gave in over submarine refuelling rights. He also agreed to joint military talks about a proposed German-Spanish attack on Gibraltar. But nothing came of it; Franco wanted the Rock for himself. However, when Hitler agreed to Franco's claim that French colonial territories be

added to Spain's North African colonies, the
Generalissimo agreed to modify the Spanish status in
the war from one of neutrality to "non-belligerence".
He also agreed to send a token Spanish military
contribution to support the Nazis. Known as the "Blue
Division", the Spanish troops were commanded by
General Munoz Grandes and were later sent to the
Russian front and slaughtered by the Soviet army.

Franco was clearly boxing clever. He was skilled at
balancing one group against another. The line-up in
the *junta* showed that the generals with monarchist
leanings were less pro-Nazi than the Falangists.
Franco's War Minister, General Varela, was conserva-

Above The famous meeting
between Adolf Hitler and
Francisco Franco on 12th
October, 1940. Afterwards Hitler
is reported to have said he'd rather
have two teeth out than go
through it again.

tive and openly pro-British, as was the Navy Minister, Admiral Moren. The Air Minister, General Yague, was fanatically pro-Nazi. So, too, was the powerful Minister for Home Affairs, Ramon Serrano-Suner, Franco's brother-in-law. The anti-Nazi wing was significantly strengthened when Franco sent Munoz Grandes off to war with the Blue Division. Suner was then shifted from Home to Foreign Affairs. There were also other signs that Franco was prepared to balance obvious pro-German pressure with "back door" openings for the western allies. An "Iberian Bloc" was set up in February 1942. It formalized and extended the agreement already existing between the Portuguese and Spanish dictators. The objective of the new bloc was to co-ordinate foreign policy and preserve the independence and neutrality of the whole peninsula.

Portugal's position as Britain's "oldest ally" did not escape notice in Spain. Another aspect of Franco's facing-both-ways policy was the Spanish attitude to the Allies' "underground" railway over the Pyrenees to Spain. Prisoners of war, helped by anti-Nazi resistance groups in France, were escaping over the mountainous frontier and surrendering to the Spanish authorities for imprisonment. But a system had started to operate which enabled prisoners of war to be repatriated to North America as long as Spain's wheat supplies had a safe passage through the Allies' anti-Nazi naval blockade.

Nazi counterpressure showed itself again when Falangists started demonstrating against ministers known to be sympathetic to the Allies. A serious clash took place between young Carlists (monarchists) and Falangists when General Varela visited Bilbao. Shots were fired and grenades exploded. The army was angry. Falange provocation was denounced. Generals Varela and Aranda saw Franco and demanded Suner's dismissal. But Varela himself was dismissed. So was

General Galarza, another service minister. Suner, however, was sacked from the Foreign Office.

The United States intervened decisively to consolidate Franco's balance of control. A secret note was delivered to the Caudillo by the American ambassador after the US entered the war in 1941. It was a personal note from President Roosevelt, delivered on the eve of the Anglo-American invasion of North Africa. The letter promised Allied respect for Spain's territorial integrity and non-intervention in Spain's internal affairs. Franco mobilized the Moroccan army during the invasion. But it remained stationary during the Allied operations. Roosevelt had virtually ensured the survival of the Franco regime.

A new situation developed after the war. Had Franco been too clever? He hoped Britain would respect his policy of "hands off Gibraltar" but he received no agreement from London. He was firmly told "Gibraltar remains British". Nor was there a welcome for Spain at the United Nations. Franco was firmly classed with the defeated fascists. So Spain faced an international boycott. There was no investment help nor was Marshall Aid forthcoming. Even more disturbing for Franco was the possibility of renewed international antifascist pressure. Ardent Spanish antifascists were flooding back across the mountains using the underground Allied escape route. French resistance fighters brought their weapons with them.

Franco again changed his tune. The pro-Nazi Falange were no longer in favour. The pro-Allied army leaders came back. These generals were also monarchists. In fact, a number of generals had previously petitioned Franco in 1942 to restore the monarchy. But he had stalled them by revealing Roosevelt's pledge, and had warned of economic difficulties and a lack of popular support for restoration. But the Monarchist solution could still offer a way out.

11. Bitter Harvest

Below A popular drawing of Franco on a gate post.

At the end of the Second World War Spain and Franco were the outcasts of Europe. The country was increasingly isolated from the outside world. The General was under pressure. He was obsessed with the possibility of antifascist intervention from outside and also desperately needed to re-assert his authority within Spain itself.

Franco attempted to give his administration a face lift, to make it more acceptable as a candidate for US economic aid, in spite of the international boycott. He went for more "catholic appeal". He brought in a so-called Catholic Action leader, Señor Alberto Martin Artajo, as Foreign Minister. He down-graded the Falange and dropped some monarchists. The reshuffle was not entirely convincing. However, it blocked the royalists' intrigues for an immediate restoration of the monarchy to get in ahead of any external influences on the right.

Once again Franco had proved his political mastery. He had consistently demonstrated his skill at papering over cracks in the coalition since the Burgos coup in 1936 when he emerged as *el Caudillo*. His first effective action then had been to knock together the heads of the monarchist factions and the Falange. They had been told to unite as a national fascist movement. The Monarchist leader, the Marqués Fal Conde, had been packed off to exile in Portugal. Disobedient Falange leaders, such as Manuel Hedilla, were singled out for harsh disciplinary treatment. The Leader had decreed Spain to be a "Nationalist Syndicalist state" in August 1937. The new *Falange Española Tradicionalista* (FET) had been formed at the same time.

The FET was conceived as a wide national party open to all supporters of the regime, rather than a narrow cult of super-stars. But it was still committed to the usual fascist mixture of race theory, imperialist glorification, national union (under dictatorship) and a corporate state system of national trade union groups, supposedly to control social and economic policy. The Nationalist Syndicalist system, in fact, proved to be a characteristic fascist device for keeping workers in line through government-controlled organization.

There were other instances of Franco's sense of political self-protection. During the ups and downs of the European war he re-introduced a sort of National Assembly. The new Cortes was strictly controlled. Every member was screened and nominated by state organizations or "voted" in by the corporations. An equally suspect Bill of Rights was also proclaimed. Under tight state control, it paid little attention to civil liberties. In reality little was done to lighten the toughness of the new inquisition introduced by the police state. Everything was controlled. Censorship was rigid and even the names of bars, hotels and restaurants were censored. The list of banned books was even longer than the official Catholic Index.

The General's complete and rigorous control over all political, intellectual and social affairs was matched by a notable lack of effective economic control or direction. Spain had reverted to conditions of semi-feudal underdevelopment, similar to those existing before the Republic. In 1940, Franco himself had conceded things were in a bad way and that it would take five years before things got back even to what they had been in 1935. In fact it took more than ten years. The desperate poverty of this period known as "the Starvation" lasted even longer. Life for most ordinary people in Spain after the Civil War was hell.

"During the years 1942-44, Spain became the scene of an economic tug-of-war between German and Anglo-American exporters who vied for the purchase of Spanish pyrites and tungsten vital to munition making. The Spanish government export commissions sold to the highest bidder, driving prices to previously unimaginable heights." *Stanley Payne,* Franco's Spain.

Above After the civil war food became very scarce. Madrid housewives search the city's rubbish dumps for scraps to feed their families.

Unemployment was reaching staggering heights. Conditions for the peasants—the majority of the population—were intolerable. Impoverished gangs scavenged in fields and rubbish heaps for anything they could find. A vast horde of ragged, jobless people wandered around from town to town. Insanitary, unsightly shanty-towns grew up on the outskirts of the cities. They were a standing reminder of the horrors of the police state. Survival in such conditions was a lottery. One of the "lost boys" of the period who made it was Manuel Benitez, or *El Cordobes,* Spain's greatest living bullfighter.

It was obvious that political tensions were being generated in spite of strict security centres and harsh police action. The 1942 tensions between the army and the Falange had reflected other dangerous undercurrents. It suited the pro-Nazi Suner to exploit them. Franco's ambitious brother-in-law also stood to gain. He had taken care to promote and organize the *Auxilio Social,* the only social service organization in the country. However meagre and restricted its benefits, the movement was an instrument for boosting his political popularity. It was modelled on the Nazi "Winter Help". The movement at first seemed to revive

Below Thousands of people were made homeless after the civil war, and "shanty towns" grew up on the outskirts of the cities. This photograph shows how some families were forced to live in Barcelona.

> "The Archbishop of Seville denounced the Falange as an instrument of materialistic totalitarianism yet at the same time demanded tighter moral censorship and the absolute elimination of all Protestantism in Spain. He denounced the 1953 agreement with the 'relativist' United States as Godless backsliding, the selling of the national birthright for a mess of pottage." *Stanley Payne,* Franco's Spain.

memories, now almost faded beyond recall, of the Falange's initial concern with social justice and mass action. But the Falange was distrusted by the Catholic hierarchy as a potential destructive influence. At one time Cardinal Segura bitterly denounced the movement as "a pagan abomination more dangerous to religion than Communism". The Cardinal's comments reflected the Church's determination to re-establish complete domination over the minds if not the bodies of the people.

On the economic front Franco showed a complete disregard for any form of planning or control. The fact was that the General's overwhelming political and military victory had been followed by an unrestrained free-for-all among the enemies of the Republic, the stock figures of capitalist society: the bankers, financiers, dispossessed landowners, speculators, mine-owners and industrialists. The financial backers of the fascist and clerical fascist movements of the 1930s came flocking back.

Naturally Juan March was among them. This astute businessman from Majorca had been granted a tobacco monopoly in the early 1930s. He was also a director of the Rio Tinto copper mines. Now, he returned to acquire monopoly control over all Spanish trade with Britain. It seemed to be his reward for financing the launching of the Falange.

The monopolists were in control throughout the 1940s. An economic survey in 1953 revealed that in every sphere of production — mining, industry, agriculture, banking — a small group of wealthy organizations completely dominated and controlled the majority of smaller enterprises. The black market also flourished. Anything could be bought for a price. Corruption was everywhere. Smuggling accounted for nearly one-third of the total annual imports into the country.

In 1956 the official Falange newspaper, *Arriba,*

summed up the country's economic state. 14 per cent of the population enjoyed 42 per cent of the national income. Some 5½ million people were earning less than £10 a week. Only 100,000 earned £5,000 or more a year. Spain, it was admitted, was on the verge of total bankruptcy. Something had to be done.

Above The Rio Tinto Copper Mine at Huelva, in Southern Spain. The photograph shows a general view of the Atalaya open-cast mine which forms part of the Rio Tinto workings.

12. Rising Hopes

The "cold war" period, when relationships between the antifascist allies of the Second World War froze into positions of mutual suspicion and hostility, offered General Franco an opportunity he could not afford to ignore. But he still had to overcome bitter hostility in Europe as a former ally of Hitler and Mussolini. Not even the post-war tensions during the twelve years or so after 1945 had any appreciable influence in breaking the general European boycott of fascist Spain.

It was not considered appropriate for fascist Spain to be included in the European Defence Community; nor was General Franco invited to join the North Atlantic Treaty Organization (NATO) which succeeded it. Economically, Spain obtained none of the initial financial or other forms of help that the United States was liberally handing out in Europe under the plan devised by General Marshall, formerly Supreme Allied Commander in Europe, then US Secretary of State. General Franco was forced to seriously consider what could be done to guarantee his country some benefit from the Marshall Plan.

In 1947 he took a hesitant first step to make it seem that the Spanish people were, at last, again being consulted on some aspect of Franco's policy. They were asked to vote in a national decree to approve a new "Law of Succession". The regime was actually being institutionalized. It was redefined as a kingdom under a dictator, acting as a Regent. A Council of State was established to assist the Chief of State. There was also a special three-man Regency Council due to function if anything happened to incapacitate the Caudillo. General Franco, of course, nominated everyone. He nominated the Council and he also retained the right to nominate his successor. The function of the Regency Council, consisting of the President of the Cortes, the most senior Cardinal Archbishop, and the most senior Army General, was solely to supervise the change-over.

The Law of Succession was obviously a wise precaution in view of General Franco's advancing years. But it was not very positive evidence of the emergence of any democratic spirit in the regime. The move, however, had important repercussions. It was apparently sufficiently significant to justify the late President Juan Peron of the Republic of Argentine, making a State visit to Spain in 1947, with his first wife. The visit broke the international boycott of Spain. It may also have paved the way for even more significant developments to come from North America. The fact was that the United States was then forcefully scouring the world for opportunities to extend its land and airbases against alleged Soviet aggression. Thus, General Franco found himself in a position to exploit his unquestionable anti-communist bias to obtain, as a "cold war warrior", the economic aid he had been unable to get for having been a fascist ally. In return, President Truman succeeded, in two years, in getting out of the Spanish leader concessions which Hitler had failed to obtain throughout the whole of the Second World War.

In 1953 Franco agreed to a ten-year Treaty of Military Assistance and Economic Aid with the United States. It granted the United States the right to build three major strategic bomber command bases and a naval base in the south of Spain. The military and economic aid began to mount up. By 1965 it was reckoned to have reached something like £400 million.

"Manolo Benitez and Juan Horillo's emigration from Palma to Madrid in 1956 was forced, but it symbolized none-the-less the effect of life in their nation in the decade of the nineteen-fifties. Three million others, like them, one Spaniard in ten, left their homes in that period, forced elsewhere in a desperate search for work. By the thousands they had, like Manolo and Juan, poured into Madrid. These reluctant emigrants clustered in a series of ramshackle encampments outside the capital, the squalid settlements thronging Madrid like a scar tissue. The huts were thrown together of wattled sheets of rusting metal, packing cases, cinder blocks stolen from construction sites. . . ." *L. Collins and D. Lapierre,* Or I'll Dress You in Mourning.

The Americans were shocked at the conditions they found in Spain. Field investigators discovered widespread corruption and official incompetence everywhere they went. Something like a third of Spain's total annual imports were actually coming into the country illegally, while huge quantities of goods were being smuggled across the Pyrenees. Some of the most active smugglers were found to be officials and members of the armed forces. Officers were reported to be customs-dodging on a large scale. They even dared customs inspectors to examine bags crammed with watches, radios, record-players and typewriters on pain of death.

Spain's transport system was another scandal. Spanish roads were notorious throughout Europe. Up-to-date motorways were non-existent. Even alleged first-class or main roads were frequently little more than cart tracks. The railway network was equally

Below One of the American airbases built in Spain following the agreement in 1953 to set up a Treaty of Military Assistance and Economic Aid between Spain and the US.

deficient. Far-reaching modernization was needed urgently if Spain was to meet the requirements of US strategic objectives. One example discovered by US army officers showed how far behind the rest of Europe Spain was lagging in terms of fuel consumption. The new large B54 aircraft to be accommodated at the Spanish bases consumed more fuel in a single afternoon than the entire Spanish rail network consumed in a month.

The military negotiators also recognized that definite improvements in the Spanish domestic set-up were vital for the stability of relations. External pressure was exerted on Franco to take effective steps towards improving the internal economy of the country. The International Monetary Fund and the United States government agreed to help only if Franco completely adjusted his economic ideas and approved far-reaching changes inside his administration. The transformation began with the emergence into the open of a hitherto little-known Catholic organization of laymen known as "Opus Dei".

Few people knew much about Opus Dei when it first began acquiring prominence in Spanish affairs. It was a catholic lay order originating in Aragon as far back as the late 1920s. It had begun acquiring a reputation in the 1950s as a morale-boosting movement concerned with the study and application of some of the more advanced techniques for economic and social development. It had developed into an advanced group of modern-thinking specialists concerned with contemporary problems and solutions. Opus Dei was particularly concerned about the social evils of the regime coupled with its lack of economic progress. The movement had become a sort of hidden clerical opposition to the worst abuses, crude brutality and incompetence of the fascist police state. But its attitudes, also, were authoritarian, élitist and religious.

The Opus Dei movement had deliberately set out to infiltrate and recruit support in political, economic and cultural circles throughout Spain. Its influence was most marked in the universities, industry and economics. This was leading to the emergence of a new breed of modern Spanish technocrat. Politically, the movement seemed inclined towards the opposition monarchists and army circles. But its biggest impact was in the field of economic expansion and industrial development. In 1957 Opus Dei was clearly on the way up. Members were given jobs in a government re-shuffle. They increased their influence even further in later cabinet changes in 1962 and 1965. In contrast, a number of Falange ministers were dropped. Even more significant was the increasingly obvious lack of public support for the only political movement in the country. There was a dramatic fall in membership and it was accused of being a minority party even among supporters of the system.

Attempts had been made to revive flagging support for the Falange after student clashes at Madrid University the previous year. Party agitators had been getting prepared for new, stronger, anti-student actions. Liberals were to be "liquidated". Franco was forced to intervene and demand restraint. The Falange was told to reorganize itself. An old reliable, José Luis de Arrese, was appointed Secretary-General to give the movement a new image and a more "progressive" programme. But when a special Falange congress came up with far-reaching new suggestions, Franco vetoed the lot. Among the proposals were suggestions for "free elections" to the Cortes (provided voters were members of the organization), the appointment of a Prime Minister, and Government responsibility to Parliament.

In spite of the evident presence of popular feeling there were few signs that the General was prepared to give up his supreme powers. He always counted on the

> "Spanish women had also reverted to their previous status. No woman dared smoke on the streets. An Argentinian girl was arrested in Madrid for wearing slacks on the Gran Via. She was fined for 'creating a scandal on the public way'. Two-piece bathing suits were illegal. Even men were banned from wearing trunks alone. The length of women's skirts was rigorously controlled. The Guardia Civilia had rulers to measure their length. They even did it to visitors at seaside resorts. Women in shorts and slacks were liable to be insulted and attacked. In Valencia women members of Catholic Action stoned tourists after rumours that there were unmarried couples holidaying together. They tried to burn down the hotel where the offenders were supposed to be staying. The Cardinal Archbishop of Spain indicated his personal attitude by stopping his car in front of two English visitors. He roundly upbraided them for wearing sleeveless dresses in the streets of his diocese." *Richard Kisch,* They Shall Not Pass.

army to counter-balance the Falange or any other opposition, if the need arose. And he had had surprisingly little trouble with the army. It had been increasingly content over the years to satisfy itself with its professional role. Of course, many of the senior generals had personal relations with the Caudillo and had, from time to time, played significant political roles as individuals. But the army as such seemed to have lost the sense of political identity which had led the Old Guard to play such a devastating role in the defeat of the Republic. It made little difference to the country, for the gap left by their apparent political apathy had been partly filled by the new-type technocrats of Opus Dei.

In 1959 Franco was persuaded to accept new concepts of economic planning and production. The Stabilization Plan was produced. It was the model for future and even more ambitious four-year economic plans. It seemed almost as if Franco had entered what some have called the "post-ideological age", dropping the major political emphasis of the regime in favour of steady industrial advance and economic expansion. The International Monetary Fund experts and US Treasury officials were there to approve the programme. Huge new development loans were made available. Spain was on the verge of the biggest economic upsurge in its history. Unemployment dropped and investment increased. So did wages, though not as much as profits. The road system was vastly improved and a new flood of tourists poured into the country from all over Europe.

Franco was now seventy. He remained an aloof, remote personality. When he travelled through the country he used a black Rolls Royce accompanied by a small motorcycle escort of red-bereted security guards. Few attempts on his life had been admitted, although a cryptic announcement once revealed that he had

Above Franco rides in his bullet-proof car during a military parade in Madrid. The car was a present from Adolf Hitler.

suffered some minor injury in a "hunting" accident.

Franco remained the uncrowned King of Spain. He was still the man at the top. In 1970 he announced that his successor would be Don Juan Carlos, grandson of the former King Alfonso, and son of the former Pretender, Don Juan. But never at any stage was there a serious sign that the nominated prince would be anything more than a convenient puppet in his master's pocket.

13. Exit the Army Man

In the 1970s Spain was again on the threshold of dramatic changes. The Franco interregnum between the Republic and a new uncertain monarchy was clearly coming to an end. Francisco Franco was an old man. He had already lost much of his early bounce and build. He was no longer a middle-aged napoleonic figure running to fat. He seemed to have shrunk with age; his neck was scraggy; his nose was more pronounced; his eyes watered though he still managed to enjoy his favourite exercise — shooting. He also had a heart condition and varicose veins.

The General remained an aloof and rather retiring person. He avoided highly-publicized personal appearances nor did he encourage personal publicity. He was not a notable patron of sports nor was he, to any great degree, responsible for the marked decline of the popularity of bull-fighting and the subsequent growth of the popularity of football.

The Caudillo seems to have preferred the life of a country squire surrounded by his dogs and guns. He had never been a glamorous personality. He was not an inspiring public speaker and seldom indulged in violent emotional haranguing like Adolf Hitler or Benito Mussolini. His public statements were carefully phrased and usually read from well-prepared texts. He disliked paperwork and left administrative decisions to others. He remained, always, what his sister-in-law had spitefully called "just an army man".

Below El Caudillo in 1973.

Below General Franco with Prince Juan Carlos.

Franco was never the effective cultural leader of nationalist Spain. His personal influence on the arts was negligible. He showed little interest in music and disliked so-called "modern" painters. In his early days he had nourished limited literary ambitions of his own and produced a couple of "slim volumes" of verse and the script of a scenario, all devoted to the glorification of Spain and its traditions. He had also, of course, received a number of honorary degrees from Spanish universities. Franco was content to leave the conduct of artistic and moral affairs in the hands of those who claimed superior rights—the Church and the fascist Falange movement. There were, however, indications that the winds of change had already started blowing through the country to their disadvantage.

The restoration of the monarchy had always been Franco's secret ambition, however tempered by the needs of the moment. In spite of this—or perhaps because of it—The Leader also showed a marked unwillingness to give up even the smallest amount of personal power, however noble his intentions. A definite reluctance to make way for younger men had been a notable feature of the declining years of Winston Churchill in Britain, de Gaulle in France, and Konrad Adenauer in West Germany.

The Caudillo was different in so far as he managed, almost to the end, to keep his fingers firmly fixed on the levers of state power. He remained an absolute autocrat in principle, but in practice a decisive feature of his authority was that he had remained what he had always been among his key supporters, the senior officer in command. In other words Franco's authority resided in the fact that his position was acknowledged and reinforced by all the senior officers of the Spanish armed forces.

Franco had always exercised the prerogatives of power with sufficient initiative and ruthlessness to ensure that a balance was always maintained between possible rivals for his position. On his way to supreme power he had been the individual to benefit most from the convenient disappearance from the scene of some who might not always have remained so tolerant of Franco.

It was, however, a notable feature of Franco's rule that it seems to have been remarkably free from bitter internal intrigues and conspiracies threatening his personal position. Again, the indications suggest that he successfully retained power because he was able to satisfy the personal aspirations, and possibly the greed, of the various elements of the fascist regime best positioned to support him.

Franco had already gone part of the way towards arranging the circumstances of a royal restoration in the kingdom of Spain. He had designated as his successor, and future king, the young Prince Juan Carlos, the grandson of the former King Alfonso, who had been forced to abdicate in 1931. The young man had been taken under Franco's wing and carefully groomed to take over in an emergency, possibly as Regent under the procedure formulated by the Caudillo in the 1947 Law of Succession. Don Carlos had always appeared as an amiable nonentity without giving any indication of having a personality or views of his own. There were few signs of any enthusiasm among the Spanish public for the future King, or desires for the restoration of the Monarchy.

The problem of the restoration had been complicated by General Franco's calculated refusal to come to terms with Don Juan, the eldest son of King Alfonso, who claimed a prior right over his son to be recognized as the future lawful King of Spain. Franco distrusted and disliked Don Juan who, as the natural heir to the throne had, apparently, been involving himself too openly with the underground monachist groups in Spain to please the fascist leader. At one stage in the 1960s he had been associated with political moves to establish a broad alliance between all the political elements of the former Republic living abroad. This included monarchists, religious conservatives and various liberal groups as well as representatives of the trade union and left wing political movements. Even the former pro-fascist Gil Robles, by now a refugee from the Franco regime, had associated himself with the move. But negotiations failed and a popular alliance for the restoration of democracy only came into existence again in the aftermath of Franco's death.

The balance sheet of Spain's development during the last twenty years of the Franco regime showed, however, that a major transformation had taken place in many areas of the national economy. By 1972 a country which had produced its first complete automobile only in 1954 was on its way to turning out half a million cars a year. The mass production of consumer goods and household items was expanding rapidly. Spain was producing television sets, refrigerators, motor-scooters, mopeds, and a large variety of electrical equipment and household appliances. There were also signs of improved social services and benefits. There was even the beginning of a national health service.

In the sphere of social and cultural affairs there had also been adjustments. Books and magazines which only a few years back had been automatically banned were beginning to reappear. The works of internationally accepted authors, even known anti-fascists, were allowed to circulate. The works of writers like Ernest Hemingway, Jean-Paul Sartre, James Joyce and J. B. Priestley were taken off the banned list. Press censorship had been formally lifted in April 1966 by the Minister of Information, the moderate Manuel

Below The making and exporting of sherry is one of Spain's traditional industries. Here the grapes are being trodden in Jerez de la Frontera, in the sherry country of Southern Spain.

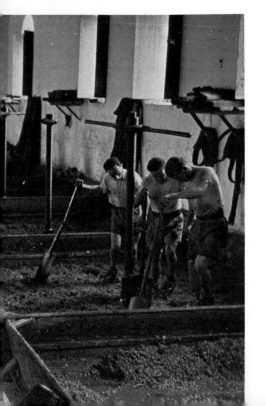

Fraga Iribarne. But there was still a so-called "fundamental law of morality", leaving publishers, editors and writers subject to arbitrary or even retrospective penalties.

In the area of education Spain remained backward. Its illiteracy rate remained the highest in Europe. Its schools lacked sufficient funds, buildings, equipment and staff. Modern teaching methods were only being adopted very slowly. Private education was the preserve of the rich and privileged. Although there had been an expansion of universities, it was still extremely difficult for the children of the under-privileged to obtain places. In spite of highly publicized plans for building new technical colleges there was very little technical education.

Spain was also suffering from galloping inflation. It was deeply in debt to the tune of some $150 million. Some of the world's great multi-national corporations had moved in to dominate its economy. It was reckoned that foreign capital accounted for 40 per cent of Spain's automobile industry and 30 per cent of its chemical industry. The huge expansion of its tourist industry had been encouraged by the inflation which followed the massive injections of external finance. Wages and living conditions for industrial workers had improved only very slowly. It was estimated that as the cost of living rose the increase of wages amounted to only half, while their real value had, of course, dropped much more. Agricultural workers were even worse off. Although over a third of Spain's total labour force was employed on the land, agricultural workers received less than a quarter of the national income. Peasant living conditions may have shown some improvement but it remained a fact that their general standard of living in no way compared with that of the townspeople.

Spain was still a very underdeveloped country.

Below Despite the great political upheavals Spain has undergone this century, for some Spaniards life has changed little. Here a swineherd tends his pigs.

Industrial tensions and social pressures were continually coming to the surface. The basic opposition to the fascist regime of the Caudillo remained strongest where it had always been, in the industrial field and among the supporters of the regional movements, particularly among the Basque and Catalan people of the north. There were signs that the old Republican opposition was beginning to revive. It showed itself in strikes and other forms of unrest. The increase in the number of strikes had been particularly noticeable among the workers of the industrialized north.

A secret trade union movement had been established paralleling the official hand-picked state organization of so-called syndicates. This had succeeded in securing and extending its authority, in spite of continued attacks from the police and security groups. Many of the industrial actions promoted and conducted by this underground trade union organization were clearly intended to demonstrate the strengh of a hidden opposition that was waiting its chance to come legally into the open. The numbers of such demonstrations had been increasing throughout the 1960s, frequently involving hundreds of thousands of workers at a time.

The last phase of Francisco Franco's life was thus dominated by the prospect of developments which might lead to the emergence of secret opposition to the fascist regime finding common cause with increasingly critical elements in the upper levels of society. These included priests as well as prelates, university teachers, lawyers and even businessmen. Many of these critics no longer bothered to hide their frustration at internal conditions in Spain. They also broadcast their resentment that Spain was still being treated as the outcast of Europe, excluded from the Common Market even though more tourists from member countries of the EEC visited Spain for their holidays than any other country. The General's frustration at not being able to

"The mountain gateways to Spain's golden shores had been thrown open. Like water rushing through a breach in a dam, a flood tide of Spain's neighbours would soon come pouring over those passes, exposing her people in one overwhelming rush to all the temptations and values from which Franco had sought to isolate them. . . ." *L. Collins and D. Lapierre,* Or I'll Dress You in Mourning.

find a solution to these difficulties had not been soothed by the fact that his chosen successor, Don Carlos, had failed to make a good impression on the Spanish people as a whole. The Caudillo had given Don Carlos a trial run at kingship during his first serious illness in July 1974. According to the Law of Succession, the Prince had been made Regent when Franco had seemed to be on his deathbed. But when the General had sufficiently recovered from the clot of blood which had been threatening his life, he quickly snatched back the authority which everyone but he had assumed to have been permanently handed over in view of his advanced age.

Then came the assassination of Admiral Carrero Blanco. On Christmas Eve 1973 a bomb exploded under the car of the Admiral, newly appointed as Prime Minister. It went off on the day when the trial was due to open in Madrid of several worker-priests and a group of suspected trade unionists accused of illegal activities. Both the car and the Admiral were blown sky-high. This act of terrorism was the signal for General Franco's last display of the vein of cruelty in his character which had seemingly been lying dormant for some years. He ordered the restoration of the garotte, a traditional Spanish instrument of execution by which the condemned person is strangled to death by means of an iron collar. In spite of world-wide reactions of horror at the proposal, the General refused to modify his position. Several men were garotted on his orders.

But Franco was nearing the end of his time. In September 1975 he was again struck by a re-occurrence of the trouble which had nearly caused his death in 1974. This time there was no hurry about handing over to the Prince. Franco, almost fiercely, seemed to be fighting hard to keep his hold, even though there was less chance than before that he would recover. He was

"Trained as a soldier but raised to be King, Prince Juan Carlos, at 36, is, after Franco, the most public but little-known figure in Spain. He is frequently seen on television—but is not heard. When he telephoned the Prado Palace after hearing of Admiral Carrero Blanco's assassination, he was told the Generalissimo would attend the funeral, subject to medical advice. But the following day, Juan Carlos followed behind the Admiral's coffin, a lonely figure by himself." Paris-Match, *19th January, 1974.*

Below The Spanish Prime Minister Vice-Admiral Luis Carrero Blanco, who was assassinated on 20th December, 1973.

gravely ill. Although he stepped down as Head of State it was several weeks before Juan Carlos again found himself Regent.

The Caudillo lingered. His heart was kept beating by the most advanced medical procedures. Behind the scenes the men who would still be left when he was gone had plenty to worry about. The signs of a prolonged struggle for the future of Spain could be identified. When Francisco Franco finally died on 20th November, 1975, Don Juan Carlos was proclaimed King of Spain almost immediately. Francisco Franco had thus, after his death, achieved his life-long ambition to restore the monarchy. But who can say how long it will be maintained?

Above Franco with Prince Juan Carlos, his chosen successor.

Opposite page General Franco and his wife Dona Carmen Polo during their Golden Wedding celebrations in October, 1973.

Principal Characters

Alfonso XIII (1886-1941). King of Spain.

Arias Salgado, Gabriel. Franco's cousin. Ultra-Catholic, he introduced strict censorship and control of culture during his period as Minister of Information until 1962.

Azana, Manuel (1880-1940). Leading Liberal Republican, War Minister 1931 and Prime Minister 1931-33 and 1936. President of Spain, March 1936-March 1939.

Carlos, Don Juan (born 1938). Son of the former Habsburg-Bourbon Pretender, Don Juan; designated Prince of Spain, and heir to the monarchy, by General Franco, 1970.

Carrero Blanco, Admiral. Prime Minister appointed by Franco, 1972. Assassinated in Madrid, late 1973.

Franco, Ramon. The General's younger brother, internationally known aviator and anti-monarchist.

Goded, General Manuel. Close army colleague of General Franco, captured by Republicans, July 1936, executed for treason.

Millan Astray, General. Organizer of the notorious 3rd Division of the Spanish Foreign Legion, self-appointed scourge of uncommitted intellectuals.

Mola, General Emilio. Director of the army conspiracy against the 1936 Republic. Died in aircrash outside Madrid, 1937.

Negrin, Dr Juan. Spanish Socialist leader; last Republican Prime Minister.

Primo de Rivera, Don Antonio. Founder of the original Falange, the Spanish fascist movement.

Sanjurjo, General José. The "Lion of the Riffs", hero of the Spanish monarchy's colonial wars in Morocco; became Head of State after 1936 military rising, but died in aircrash while on his way to join the *junta*.

Serrano-Suner, Ramon. Franco's brother-in-law, ardent supporter of German and Italian fascism, leader of the Spanish Catholic fascist youth movement.

Table of Dates

1873	1st Spanish Republic proclaimed.
1881	Trade Unions legalized.
1892	Francisco Franco born, El Ferrol.
1910	Graduated 2nd Lieutenant, Toledo Infantry College.
1912	1st Moroccan campaign.
1916	Franco wounded in the stomach.
1920	Promoted to Major, and Garrison Commander, Oviedo.
1921	Re-posted to Morocco. Riff campaign.
1923	Promoted Lt-Colonel, marries Carmen Polo. Primo de Rivera becomes dictator. Spanish Foreign Legion founded.
1926	Promoted Brigadier-General.
1927	Commandant, Saragossa General Military Academy.
1928	Visits Germany.
1930	Dictatorship collapses: death of Primo de Rivera.
1931	King Alfonso XIII abdicates. 2nd Republic proclaimed.
1932	Garrison Commander, Corunna. Sanjurjo army plot fails. Franco re-posted Balearic Islands as Captain-General.
1933	Right wing election victory. Hitler takes over Germany. Italian fascists invade Ethiopia.
1934	Franco puts down Asturias miners' strike, imports Moorish troops.
1935	Franco, Chief of Staff, Army. Lerroux government falls.
1936 Feb	Popular Front government elected.
Mar	Franco exiled to Canary Islands, Captain-General.

Jul	The Generals revolt against Republic. Franco's airlift.
Sept	Non-Intervention Committee set up in London.
Oct	Franco proclaimed Supreme Commander, Nationalist forces, and Chief of State.
1937	Franco decree: the future National Syndicalist State; the Falange reformed into the *Falange Española Tradicionalista* (FET).
1939	Franco issues Victory communiqué.
1940	Meeting with Adolf Hitler, Hendaye, France.
1942	Iberian Bloc with Portugal.
1953	10-year Military and Economic Treaty with USA.
1957	Opus Dei enters Government.
1959	Stabilization Plan backed by 600 million dollars in foreign loans: Spain joins Organization of European Economic Co-operation.
1962	Franco's 70th birthday.
1964	Elected member General Society Spanish Authors.
1965	Right to strike concession, after 30 years.
1970	Juan Carlos declared Prince of Spain, and future King.
1973	Admiral Luis Carrero Blanco becomes first Prime Minister to be appointed by Franco.
1974	Carrero Blanco assassinated.
1975	Franco dies aged 83 years. Don Juan Carlos proclaimed King of Spain.

Further Reading

These are the only two biographies of the Caudillo published outside Spain to be approved by the Spanish Government:

Crozier, Brian. *Franco: A Biographical History* (Eyre and Spottiswood, 1967).

Hills, George. *Franco — The Man and His Nation* (Robert Hale, 1967).

Other books covering the period are:

Brenan, Gerald. *The Spanish Labyrinth* (Cambridge University Press, 1943). A far-sighted, sensitive review of twentieth-century developments in Spain, with a glance back at history, and particularly relevant assessments of agricultural and peasant development.

Brone, Pierre and Temine, Emile. *The Revolution and Civil War in Spain* (Faber, 1970). The shrewdest political appreciation of the political undercurrents and social clashes of the conflict.

Collins, L. and Lapierre, D. *Or I'll Dress You in Mourning* (Weidenfeld and Nicolson, 1968). The story of one of Spain's best-known war-babies, the great bullfighter known as El Cordobes, with much revealing background.

Fraser, Ronald. *In Hiding: the life of Manuel Cortes* (Allen Lane, 1972). The taped account of 30 years in the life of a village mayor and his family after the Civil War.

Kisch, Richard. *They Shall Not Pass* (Wayland, 1974). Surveys the social background of the Spanish people at war, 1936-39.

Payne, Stanley. *Franco's Spain* (Routledge, 1968). This remains the most concise, authoritative and objective, general history of contemporary Spain.

Thomas, Hugh. *The Spanish Civil War* (Eyre and Spottiswood, 1961). A fully documented account of the 1936-39 conflict.

Index

Picture Credits

The Author and Publisher would like to thank those who have given permission for copyright photographs to appear on the following pages: Keystone Press Agency Ltd, 6, 26, 34, 38, 39, 45, 46, 49, 55, 59, 63, 67, 78, 83, 89, 90, 91; Radio Times Hulton Picture Library, 8, 14, 16, 18 (*top, bottom left and right*), 21, 24, 30, 32, 36, 70, 73, 82, 86, 87; The Mansell Collection, *frontispiece,* 15, 22; The Spanish Embassy, London, 11; United Press International, 25, 52; Associated Press, 43, 58, 60, 61, 75; Black Star Ltd, 72, 84; The Wayland Picture Library, 29, 53.